TRULY
TEXAS
MEXICAN

TRULY TEXAS MEXICAN

A Native Culinary Heritage in Recipes

Adán Medrano

Texas Tech University Press

This book is typeset in Amasis. The paper used in this book
meets the minimum requirements of ANSI/NISO Z39.48-
1992 (R1997). ∞

Designed by Kasey McBeath
Cover photograph by Adán Medrano

Library of Congress Cataloging-in-Publication Data
Medrano, Adán, author.
    Truly Texas Mexican : a native culinary heritage in
recipes / Adán Medrano.
        pages cm. — (The Grover E. Murray studies in
the American Southwest)
    Summary: "A cookbook that explores the indigenous
culinary heritage of Texas's Mexican American community:
Includes recipes and photographs"— Provided by publisher.

Includes bibliographical references and index.
    ISBN 978-0-89672-850-9 (hardback) — ISBN
978-0-89672-851-6 (e-book) 1. Mexican American cooking.
2. Cooking, American—Southern style. 3. Cooking—Texas.
I. Title.
    TX715.2.S69M47 2014
    641.5926872073—dc23   2013045939

16 17 18 19 20 21 22 / 9 8 7 6 5 4 3 2

Texas Tech University Press
Box 41037 | Lubbock, Texas 79409-1037 USA
800.832.4042 | ttup@ttu.edu | www.ttupress.org

To *amá*, Dominga Mora Medrano
and my partner, Richard Jiménez

CONTENTS

MAPS

TRULY TEXAS MEXICAN

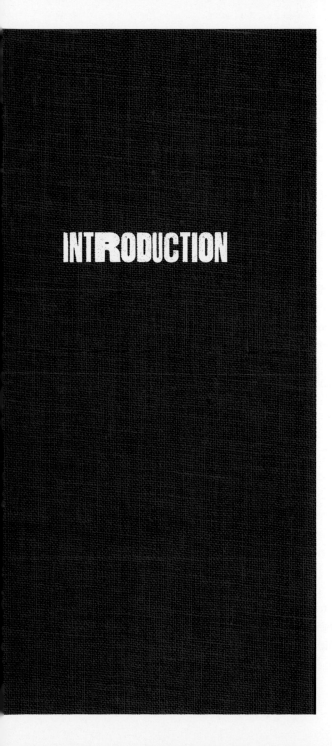

INTRODUCTION

The 100 recipes in this book represent only a small part of the rich repertoire of Texas Mexican dishes that have been taught from one generation to the next. They belong to the indigenous people who have inhabited Texas for thousands of years, mastering the selection of ingredients and the application of culinary techniques. The recipes are presented within their history, both ancient and recent, in an effort to make the dishes more enjoyable and instructive of who we are today.

I use a variety of names for our indigenous ancestors, none completely satisfactory but each describing an aspect of our reality. In Chapter 1, I explain what I mean by Texas Mexican food and locate its origins in south Texas and northern Mexico. Today the cuisine is no longer limited to this region but is enjoyed throughout the United States. I differentiate our cuisine from the so-called Tex-Mex and describe some of the differences.

In Chapter 2, I briefly outline the ten-thousand-year history of the peoples who created today's Texas Mexican cuisine. I describe the ingredients they used and the cooking techniques they developed that we still use today. I also describe some of the dishes they served, all naturally local and seasonal.

I selected these recipes because they are the most recognized as traditional to our community, the Mexican American working class. I spent my boyhood summers in the fields picking cotton, hoeing sugar beets and soybeans, picking tomatoes, watermelons, corn, okra, cherries, and apples. It was rough being economically poor, working long days, and being excluded from opportunity. Meals brought joy to our day. Cooking was an act of survival, creativity, and affirmation. To this day I enjoy those same delicious meals that my *amá* prepared so masterfully, using the scarce resources available to her (we called her *amá* instead of the Spanish *mamá*). They are cherished recipes that she learned from former generations, tested and perfected over time. As I grew up I learned the techniques from my mother and later from my sisters and brother. From my *apá* (father), I learned some of the mechanics such as digging an earth oven and making an aluminum shed for drying meat.

My initial attempts at home cooking were not as successful as my mother's. Yes, I did burn the beans badly because I could not judge the water level. I used too much fat in the potatoes and chiles. And in trying to be creative, I did venture into hideous flavor territory by adding diced apples to scrambled eggs with *chile serrano*. I urge you to never try that. But I learned to balance trial and error with having a firm understanding of the traditional, tested methods, and this helped me greatly when I enrolled in The Culinary Institute of America. Training to be a chef requires an understanding of chemistry, mastery of exacting techniques, and a strong back. I had the strong back from years of heavy manual labor, and although I was familiar with many of the chemical reactions, I was able to learn the European culinary terms for them. For example, the centuries-old technique that my mother used of slowly roasting pinto beans to develop depth of meaty flavor

and color was given the name of a French physicist who described it around 1910. The series of chemical reactions of amino acids and carbohydrate molecules when slowly roasted is called the Maillard reaction. We call it *bien guisado*, as we carefully activate the slow changes in color and texture by applying medium heat to the pinto beans while stirring and scraping. Privileged to graduate from such a prestigious culinary school, I learned to approach cuisine from different angles and gained an even greater appreciation of the importance of culture. The school helped me to focus, and now my mother's kitchen prevails as my foundation and culinary compass.

I do not include the vast array of Texas Mexican wild game dishes and the subtleties of outdoor open-fire cooking, even though they are an important part of our cuisine. Nor do I include the many offal dishes that deliciously mark our family and community celebrations (Montaño, 1992). This is because the subjects merit books unto themselves. I do, however, include several dishes that are completely new but created in the spirit of the Texas Mexican flavor profile. A dish like my watermelon ice with blueberries was never served in my childhood home, but I do prepare it today in my kitchen. This dish indicates how our cuisine is evolving and creating new combinations of European and Mesoamerican, "New World" ingredients. By including such dishes I wish to acknowledge the many innovative Mexican American chefs and cooks who feel grounded in our traditions and from that vantage point are creating new interpretations of Texas Mexican dishes, in tune with our lifestyles today.

The difficulty levels of the recipes extend from boiling water for chocolate to elaborate dishes intended for the experienced cook. I do not include dishes that are widely known but which we did not cook at home, such as crispy tacos that are offered on menus of restaurants that call themselves Tex-Mex. This book is not about Tex-Mex food.

I hope you find the recipes welcoming and the history enjoyable.

PART I:
HISTORY

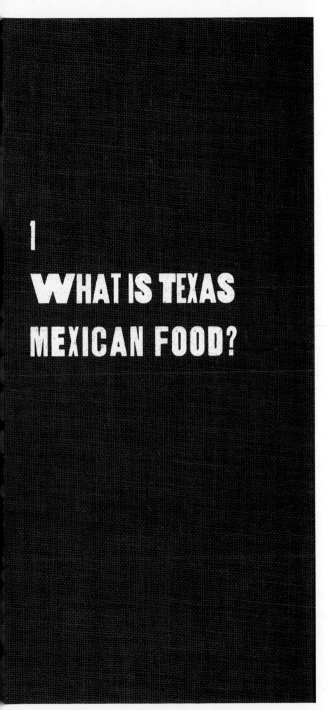

1
WHAT IS TEXAS MEXICAN FOOD?

"Texas Mexican" is the cuisine that has evolved over centuries in the region immediately north and south of the lower Rio Grande. It is deeply rooted in the indigenous cultures of what are now northeastern Mexico and central and south Texas, the region where my extended family and all my Mexican American friends live.

I was born and grew up in San Antonio, Texas. My earliest memories include trips from San Antonio to Del Rio and Eagle Pass on the Rio Grande and to Nava, Coahuila, Mexico, twenty-seven miles south of the Rio Grande. Besides our home in San Antonio, we also owned farmland and pecan orchards in Nava, Mexico. Whenever our family loaded onto our pickup truck to travel from one home to another, we greeted our relatives along the route. For us, the geographic region stretching from San Antonio down to Nava, a 188-mile drive, was one seamless land where relatives lived.

This book is about the history of the Texas Indians, that is, Native Americans, who live on this land and about the delicious food that has played a central role in our survival and nourishment. The written history of the cultures of this region begins in approximately 900 CE, the period during which anthropologists have identified distinct native communities and cultures. Historians suggest that over the next three centuries (between 900 and 1200 CE) the cultures and identities of nearly all the

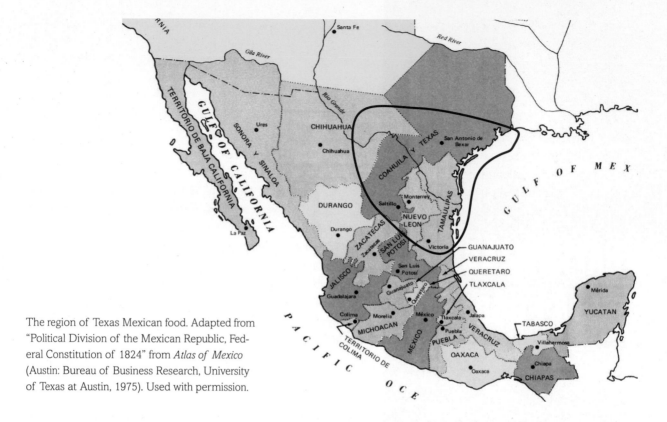

The region of Texas Mexican food. Adapted from "Political Division of the Mexican Republic, Federal Constitution of 1824" from *Atlas of Mexico* (Austin: Bureau of Business Research, University of Texas at Austin, 1975). Used with permission.

Texas Native American communities were clearly established.

Historians assert that by 1500 there were 50,000 to several hundred thousand to even a million inhabitants in Texas living in communities with diverse languages and customs (La Vere, 2004). Hundreds of names ascribed to the communities survive in Spanish documents, including Coahuiltecan, Caddo, Atakapa, and Karankawa. Their cuisine is characterized by the types of Native American ingredients shared with sister re-

gions in Mexico such as Nuevo León, Baja California, Oaxaca, Yucatán, and Jalisco. Some of these ingredients are chiles, maize, beans, tomato, potato, squash, cactus, and maguey.

However, the cuisine is also distinct from its sister regions because it developed in a geographic region with different climatic and soil conditions. Unique flavor profiles arise from the taste of river fish, seafood, flora, and fauna, which include quail, deer, turkey, clams, redfish, sotol, pecans, mesquite, and *quelite,* a variety of amaranth (*Amaranthus palmeri*). Vegetation takes on flavor characteristics of the soil in which it grows, such as the clayey or chalkish soils around San Antonio and the muddy soils of the marshy waters of the Gulf coast.

This region was the state of Coahuila y Texas, part of the Mexican Republic that claimed Texas from 1821 to 1848. It is therefore understandable that the indigenous Texas natives, along with their food, came to be known as "Mexican." But it is erroneous to locate this food history as "south of the border," for it existed also north of the Rio Grande long before it was a border. Movement back and forth from north to south of the river was continuous, seamless, not only for peaceful trade and exchange but also because of war raids and, in the 1800s, ethnic extermination policies (Anderson, 2005).

The Karankawas of Galveston Island are an example. Standing six feet tall and having lived on the coast for thousands of years they were unable to withstand the incursion and attacks of European settlers in the early nineteenth century and by mid-century were fleeing south toward the mouth of the Rio Grande and into Mexico. In 1858 almost all of them were killed in an attack by Texans.

Between 1492 and 1900, 90 percent of the native peoples of Texas died. European diseases such as cholera, smallpox, measles, and influenza devastated huge populations within weeks and even days (La Vere, 2004). The indigenous peoples who remained in Texas married into other tribes, with European settlers, and with Mexicans coming up from Southern Mexico. They sometimes lived in Catholic missions and eventually came to be known as the Mexican people of Texas. It was a process of continuous change and adaptation.

Anthropologists call this ability to survive cultural and ethnic shifts and form new cohesive identities, "ethnogenesis" (Sperry, 2007). Food production and cooking were essential to Texas Indian survival and self-identity. Faced with new circumstances, cooks had to both remember and learn anew the chemistry and nutritional makeup of the natural resources that surrounded them. Drying meat and fish had always been important to food preservation and taste and it was to continue. Earthen pits and open-fire roasting are techniques shared with civilizations all over the globe and these certainly continued. But as native cooks fled from their homelands and took shelter in Catholic missions or in newly established European towns, they encountered new animals such as pigs, cattle, and goats, and new bulbs such as garlic and onion, and could no longer depend on their traditional hunting, fishing, gathering, and gardening. Renewed culinary invention and creativity were required. From the sixteenth century to the twentieth century, their cuisine would evolve quite remarkably, even deliciously (!), and begin a new phase that would marry Texas indigenous cuisine with European dishes. These are the origins of today's Texas Mexican cuisine. Its history is dynamic and it is at home in central, coastal, and south Texas. From this place of origin the cuisine has traveled and is enjoyed today in places as varied as the Pilsen neighborhood of Chicago, South Central Los Angeles, and Seattle (Montaño, 2013).

11

Understanding how we inherited techniques from cooks in the distant to not-so-distant past heightens the joy of cooking. The tools associated with Texas Mexican food have an ancient history. In Marble Falls, north of San Antonio, archaeologists have uncovered local granite mortars dating back thousands of years. Another mortar—the *molcajete*—made of volcanic rock rather than local granite, traveled through trade routes northward from Mesoamerica and was shared by all indigenous communities along the way. That is why this highly efficient mortar is ubiquitous in the entire region all the way from Galveston, Texas, to Guatemala. You will want to have this tool in your kitchen, for it will efficiently grind spices and chiles to a paste that is fine and velvety beyond what a typical blender or food processor made for home use can achieve.

Knowing the history of ingredients can make food more delicious because a greater appreciation of the plants, nuts, grains, fish, and mammals that for thousands of years have grown naturally around us makes us more intelligent and versatile cooks. Dried chile, corn *masa*, and avocados are great ingredients, but they become part of a sumptuous dish when one understands how to devein and purée chiles, how to store masa before it sours, and how to cut open an avocado at the peak of its flavorful oils.

Cuisine as a Strategy for Community

Texas Indians underwent colossal changes when the Europeans entered their homelands and took possession. Over a period of four hundred years much of the land was taken by the Europeans who claimed ownership by means of written decrees from the king of Spain, or from the power centers of the Mexican Republic and later from the Texas Republic's European settlers (Lang and Long, 2012).

Facing these social upheavals, together with terrifying diseases and wars, our ancestors were nonetheless subjects and creators of their destinies as they found ways of adapting to new, dangerous situations. In the process they created strategies not only for survival but also for strengthening and expanding their community. How food played a key role in our ongoing identity is a fascinating part of our history.

Having lost our land and language along with economic and political standing, we continued to adapt, stepping into a new time and inventing strategies that would prove effective in the continuation and celebration of a people. Food was the cultural activity that held us together. Cooking nurtured our remembering and through it we invented new identities rooted in that remembering. Preparing food was a day-by-day regeneration. As we faced change, we also prepared and served meals to the diverse cultures that we would constantly encounter. Over time, cooks invented techniques to marry native ingredients with those of the immigrant Europeans, the result being an evolving, ever creative and unique cuisine. It was also the basis for new opportunity and new community.

Ours was a culinary strategy to prepare a meal for all whom we were to encounter—hospitality with no limits. Interesting and tasteful things began to happen in the earthen and stone ovens. Our food preparation prior to 1500 had included the use of nut oils, fish oils, and fat from some mammals, so it was a familiar step to incorporate European pork and lard into cooking native corn staples like gorditas and tamales.

I am not in agreement with some food writers who claim that our cuisine was less flavorful before the Europeans arrived and that the Spanish introduction of foreign ingredients improved the local food. Of course, our cuisine changed after the sixteenth century, but there is no evidence that it was less delicious before then. Two examples will make this clear.

I encounter a common misunderstanding that Europeans introduced fat into our cooking and thus improved our cuisine. There is plentiful historical evidence that in both Mexico and Texas, indeed in all of the Americas, we used fat in our cooking thousands of years before the arrival of Europeans (Morell and Enig, 2000). Nuts, fish, bears, beavers, and other mammals were sources. It was the specific fat from pigs—lard—that the Spaniards introduced into our cuisine.

A second common misunderstanding is that without lard, our food, and particularly the tamal, was dry and uninteresting. Surviving documents that depict Mesoamerican life before 1500, like the Codex Mendoza and the writings of Fray Bernardo de Sahagún, show that tamales were eaten at home, enjoyed at communal celebrations, and sold at markets, and that they were delicious. Sahagún makes a reference to taste when he describes the various fillings and styles of this culturally important food: "Otros tamales comían que son muy blancos y muy delicados. . . . [Y] la que es buen oficial hácelos bien hechos y sabrosos y limpios" (Garibay, 2006). (They ate other tamales which were white and

very delicate. . . . [A]nd she who is good at her work makes them well and delicious and clean.) Sahagún does describe some tamales that are dry and tasteless, but he ascribes these to deceptive sellers in the market who try to pass them off as good tamales, but they are so old and rotten as to be worthless (Berdan and Anawalt, 1977).

The subtleties of technique are handed down from one generation to another and unfortunately there is little understanding of Texas Mexican cuisine outside the homes of Mexican American families, most still economically poor. But go inside one of these homes and one will find that, similar to corn tortillas, which have no fat at all, tamales will be uninterestingly dry only if the cook dries them out. Corn masa absorbs moisture naturally and an experienced cook will use that property to good advantage. I think a good cook will serve you a bad, dry tamal only if she or he does not like you.

Actually, a delicious dry tamal does exist—the roasted tamal. My *amá* would rekindle our appetites for leftover tamales by slowly roasting them on a *comal* (griddle), charring the husk and even part of the tamal itself. For us, specks of charred black on the husk and smoky *masa* aroma rising were a real treat. I mention this technique in my tamal recipes in an effort to share what is known inside our homes.

As a contemporary chef of Texas Mexican cuisine, I think we have yet to explore the many avenues of taste that our cuisine offers. I find great joy in connecting with my culinary history. When I traveled to Oxford from London two years ago, I was thrilled to see firsthand the Codex Mendoza, which is currently the property of the Oxford Bodleian library. The illustrations by Aztec artists fascinated me, for I could almost smell the steam in the pictographs rising from platters of tamales. We need to expand our minds and our taste for history.

As part of the blending of European products into pre-existing foods, we incorporated wheat flour as a thickener, mixing it with chiles and spices. All in all, the encounter with new cultures was a culinary process that managed to create delicious and beautiful harmonies between local and foreign spices. *Carne con chile* a.k.a. *chile con carne* (recipe page 105), is a prime example of this harmony of spices, since the success of the dish depends on the foreign ingredients of cumin, black pepper, garlic, onion, and beef serving as a sumptuous backdrop to the carefully selected array of chiles, each chile offering a distinctive flavor.

The Distinction between "Tex-Mex" and Texas Mexican Cuisine

In the early 1900s, Texan Anglo entrepreneurs developed a unique variation of Texas Mexican cuisine in restaurants that catered solely to Anglo customers. These were restaurants by Anglos for Anglos with the intent of providing food that was less spicy but could still be marketed as an authentic experience of Mexican food. Not only the food, but also the restaurant décor represented an Anglo tourist's perspective of "Mexican."

Selling prepared food is an ancient Mexican tradition. Surviving native documents record that prepared foods were a feature of markets in Tlatelolco, Mexico, founded in 1338. Cooks served tamales, tortillas, *atole* (drink made from corn flour), beans, chocolate, and variously filled and stuffed tortillas (Solis and Gallegos, 2000). Ballinger, Texas was the site of a huge market fair that annually convened thousands of Texas Indians for trade in the 1400s (La Vere, 2004). I can easily imagine the likelihood of communal sharing of prepared food during these seasonal trade events.

The immediate precursors to the Tex-Mex restaurants of the early 1900s were a celebrated group of Mexican, Texas Indian businesswomen who in the 1800s and early 1900s operated open-air diners in San Antonio's downtown market square. American writers like Stephen Crane (*Red Badge of Courage*) wrote about their first taste of Mexican food as they sat at these diners run by indigenous Mexican women. Recalling his experience of dining in San Antonio in 1895, Crane wrote "upon one of the plazas, Mexican vendors with open-air stands sell food that tastes exactly like pounded fire-brick from Hades—chili con carne, tamales, enchiladas, chili verde, frijoles" (Jennings, 2012).

Eventually the women and their food stands were harassed and shut down by the San Antonio Health Department. As described by Jeffrey M. Pilcher, beginning in the 1880s, efforts had been made by city officials to remove the ladies and their food, even though they were an economically important part of the San Antonio tourism business. Officials instituted health regulations that required the ladies to use screens to cover their wares and even enclose their entire stands in screen mesh. The indigenous women restaurateurs were unable to meet the safety regulations, could not counter the political pressures against their businesses, and they, along with their prepared food, disappeared by 1943 (Pilcher, 2012).

Dr. Felix Almaráz, professor of history at The University of Texas at San Antonio says, "Alamo Plaza was more for Caucasians and business people, politicians. . . . [T]he chili queens were considered an eyesore because their little setups were not, they were not 'high tone'" (Silva and Nelson, 2004).

He laments, "When they were here, we didn't protect them. We didn't know that there would be bureaucrats who would come at them. And try to get them either to reform or to change or to move out. And it seems that they moved them out" (Silva and Nelson, 2004).

In 1900 a new restaurant appeared in downtown San Antonio near Alamo Plaza named "The Original Mexican Restaurant." Otis M. Farnsworth, a visitor to San Antonio from Chicago, had seen the success of small Mexican restaurants located in the west-side barrios and went on to open one for Anglos downtown where the native Mexican ladies had been having such success (Pilcher, 2012). He, and later other Anglo entrepreneurs, were able to meet the requirements of the newly instituted health regulations.

The food served in those restaurants came to be known as "Tex-Mex." Since the food was intended to cater to Anglo customers, cooks found ways to make it palatable to Anglo-European tastes. Patrons were served a limited flavor range of chiles, and of course were at home and already familiar with the use of pork

fat and lard. These restaurants also eventually switched from natural Texas Mexican cheeses to yellow-colored, industrially processed cheese made popular by James L. Kraft after he patented the process in 1916 (Ustunol, 2009). The menus of these restaurants were narrow in their offerings and did not delve into the larger repertoire of the Texas Mexican cuisine that was being cooked and enjoyed in homes at that time. In this regard they differed from the small cafés and *restaurantes* in the San Antonio west-side barrios that did serve the authentic food enjoyed in the Texas Mexican homes of the time. These traditional restaurantes have continued without interruption for many decades. Today everywhere in the economically poor west side of San Antonio, a great number of small cafés offer authentic Texas Mexican home cooking that differs from foods (generally) served in the downtown area of the city.

Tex-Mex restaurant food is characterized by heavy use of yellow processed cheeses in almost every dish and mashed beans with large amounts of fat, mainly lard. Almost all items are fried, so the techniques of slow roasting, boiling, herb stewing, and steaming are underutilized. The menus steer close to fried items that can be served with refried beans and rice. Traditional ingredients like *nopalitos* (cactus paddles) are rarely served. When nopalitos are served, they are often canned or pre-packaged, a practice that would never be allowed in a family Texas Mexican restaurant.

Other Tex-Mex restaurants opened all across the state. Some even took the same name as the one in San Antonio, although none were connected to each other in any way other than the name. So it was that

15

in Waco, Fort Worth, Houston, Galveston, and other cities, locals could dine at The Original Mexican Restaurant. Around the 1930s Mexican American male entrepreneurs, some of them likely the descendants of the original Texas Indians, also started opening up Tex-Mex restaurants in San Antonio and other cities with great success.

A New Cuisine

Any authentic cuisine, if it is truly at the heart of a community and family, is ever new and evolving. Contemporary Texas Mexican food continues the tradition of cooking with ingredients tied to this land, adapting to new contexts, and exploring new avenues of taste. It is seasonal and local, tied to the natural environment and its resources, to local economies and to changes in climate.

We renew by remembering. Before 1528 we used oils from fish, vegetables, nuts, and some mammals, including bears. Cactus, pecans, sotol (*Dasylirion wheeleri*, commonly known as desert spoon), and *quelite* are being rediscovered today by restaurant chefs and home cooks. Since we have embraced pork, onions, watermelon, and tamarind as culturally ours, we find innovative ways to enjoy them, exploring techniques of sous-vide, molecular, and raw.

We are about community and a celebratory, nourishing table. We are the Mexican American, Texas Indian, Texas Native American, Chicano chefs and cooks who choose to live on this our ancestral land and make a serious, delicious contribution to the culinary work of our ancestors. (I use the term "Chicano" to refer to a Mexican American who seeks a certain degree of cultural awareness and political activism [Paredes, 2012].) Our cooking gets its character from the *terroir*, that is, the special geography, geology, and climate of the land; from the combination of ingredients that over time have proven to be fitting; and from the cooking techniques that efficiently impart the flavor characteristic of our history.

I recognize a serving of my family's cooking because it matches what I see when I walk the land and feel the elements. My memory also gets involved. The land today is different from what it was three hundred years ago, before dramatic changes brought about by the arrival of Spaniards from the south and later the Anglo-Europeans from the east. Today it is overrun by mesquite, prickly pear, and thorny wild brush, previously found only in certain areas. Cattle, sheep, goats, and other new animals came so fast and were so numerous that they devastated the grasslands of the original prairies and savannahs. As they moved, these animals spread the seeds of mesquite and thorn-covered brush species that use greater amounts of water than grasses. The results are the invasion of most of the land by thick wild brush and the reduction of natural springs, creeks, and general water levels (Hall, 2006). Remembering how things were is not a nostalgic yearning to return. It is a history lesson pointing to consequences of the choices we make about food production and distribution. To me, it is a reminder to pay attention.

The first thing I encounter in today's landscape are the ingredients, including cactus, squash, beans, and of course, corn and a variety of chiles. Then there are the

16

History

sense and feeling one gets from just feeling the space. Direct heat. Clarity. Directness, again, from the flat, dry, rough terrain. No pretense. Appreciating distinctions in the character of each small thing and the subtleties of their differences.

I also recognize it because of particular combinations of ingredients. There is a flavor profile to our cuisine that can be described by specific combinations such as, for example, tomato with *chile dulce* (bell pepper). *Chile ancho* with cumin, garlic, and black pepper. Cilantro and lime with meats such as quail, venison, and rabbit. Tart, light cheese flavors with roasted green chiles. Green chiles with salt and tomato. Onion with tomato and chile. Roasted chiles with toasty corn tortillas. These combinations are basic and they are the building blocks for more varied dishes. Some of these combinations are ancient and some more recent with the arrival of new ingredients from Europe, Asia, and Africa. Over time they have developed as harmonious and complex blends that produce our unique flavor profile.

And finally, our dishes get their character from the culinary techniques developed over centuries in earth ovens, open fires, tree-bark bowls, granite mortars, griddles, and shell-lined steaming ovens. Our cuisine is characterized by roasting chiles, tamales, and cacti. We like to boil meats, and I think this comes from our long tradition of stone boiling, the ancient technique of adding hot rocks to an earthen cavity to boil meats, roots and vegetables over time (Dial, 2012). Drying meat and other foods was essential to survival and also flavorful. We steamed seafood, cooked in open fires and on clay griddles. All of the techniques that we use today in our kitchens come to us from long-ago cooks whose languages we no longer speak. We cook as they did.

The work that archaeologists have done in Texas deserves much more recognition and acclaim than it has received. So does the oral tradition that is at work constantly in Mexican American homes from generation to generation. From these two streams of knowledge I have learned to use a *molcajete*, and to roast, steam, griddle cook, grind, fry, and bake. I want to share with other cooks this knowledge, skill, and sense of belonging.

Conscious of the horrors of our violent history, I think that ours must be an aesthetic grounded in economic justice, the true context for peace. Most of us, the Mexican American working class, are still economically poor, the vestiges of our previous devastations. We have limited access to formal education and health care. We dream of a society better than the one from which we have come. From this position, many of us wish to be artful chefs.

It takes clarity of mind and palate to cook delicious Texas Mexican food. We develop this clarity by being true to the flavors developed by former cooks, as we laboriously learn about them and build upon them, and by being attentive to how we buy, prepare, and serve, so that we may foster awareness of justice in food production and purchasing and in wages paid to food workers.

As we are more mindful of the economic context, the land, and the environment, so will we grow in understanding the character, texture, and flavor of our

17

ingredients. It is a work of love to share the recipes in this book. Hopefully, we will continue to develop a loving finesse in our cooking techniques, an appreciation of the humanity of all who come to our table. After all, our native culinary heritage prompts us to comfort, to heal, and to enjoy.

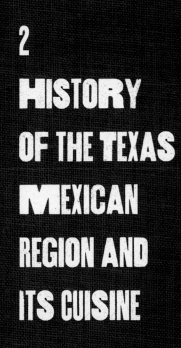

2

HISTORY OF THE TEXAS MEXICAN REGION AND ITS CUISINE

Gathering and preparing food in Texas goes back at least 13,500 years, for that is how long humans have lived here. Cooking as a distinguishable act of a specific cultural group begins in 900 CE. Between 900 and 1200 CE most indigenous communities had developed distinctive ways of societal organization, familial relationships, ceremonial rituals, methods for obtaining foodstuffs, and tools and techniques for food preparation (La Vere, 2004).

The food of our ancestors is as varied as the geography: conch, oysters, and red snapper along the coast; deer, snails, and catfish around San Antonio; rabbits, turkeys, and prickly pear cactus in the southern semi-desert. All of these comprised the resources from which cooks prepared meals for everyday sustenance, special family treats, and large community celebrations. Daily nourishment required a direct and constant relationship to the land and all its resources.

This is the land where I learned to cook and learned my family's recipes. The terroir that feeds my culinary inspiration is the central, southern, and coastal area of Texas, which is bound historically, culturally, and biologically to northern Mexico just south of the lower Rio Grande. I describe this place as the Texas Mexican triangle: imagine a line beginning in Del Rio, going east to San Antonio and Victoria and down along the coast to Brownsville, and then passing along the Rio Grande back to Del Rio.

This triangle was home to hundreds of culturally distinct indigenous communities, some as small as a dozen persons. Faced with near-annihilation following the arrival of Europeans in 1528, having lost their lands and their language, they eventually became the Mexican peasant class of the 1800s and continue as a part of the Mexican American community today (Newcomb, 1961). They not only survived, but invented a completely new identity. If you stand on any street corner in downtown San Antonio, the facial features and physical makeup of the people strike you as clearly indigenous. Speaking some Spanish but mainly English, and with extended families like mine that live on both sides of the river, we have been here longer than we can remember. As mentioned in Chapter 1, ethnogenesis is the term anthropologists use for this process of becoming anew, the remaking of oneself when confronted with foreign others in new, often destructive, circumstances (Sperry, 2007).

A common metaphor for ethnic identity is branches on a tree. The identity of the newest growth, that outermost, smallest branch, is determined by its connectedness to the larger branches and to the parent tree. Genealogical family trees are understood in this way, identity being an unbroken link to a parent group.

Some anthropologists have another way of perceiving ethnic identity. Ethnogenesis focuses on the making of ethnic identity through the metaphor of a rhizome rather than a branch (Moore, 1994).

A rhizome is the underground tubular system of certain plants that extends continuously outward laterally, and collects and stores nutrients. The cattail plant

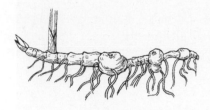

A rhizome is the underground expansive, tubular stem of certain plants that extends continuously outward, laterally, and collects and stores nutrients. (From http://www.wpclipart.com/plants/diagrams/plant_parts_2/rhizome.png.html.)

of the Texas Gulf coast has such a rhizome. The winding, tube-like rhizome spreads widely, and as it collects and stores food, it develops a great number of nodes, each of which is capable of generating a brand new plant. Another rhizome is ginger root, perhaps more familiar to cooks than the Texas cattail. One can snap the ginger root apart into nodes. If you break a rhizome apart and plant any of the broken, separated nodes in a new environment, they will each grow a sturdy new plant so long as they can find physical nourishment. The rhizome travels well to a new spot, withstands breakage, and grows cohesively, taking nourishment from its new environment and resources.

When I cook Texas Mexican food as taught to me by my mother—blending, mixing, cutting, and seasoning—it is the rhizome, not the branch, that comes to mind. My foods and identity do not depend primarily on the historic connection to a parent group, that is, connections unbroken over space and time. Instead, they are the outcome of connections established in time, ones that I make from existing memory, family relationships, resources at hand, from intuition and

History

choices. It is creative, rhizotic ethnogenesis. Only a cohesive, creative people could so successfully look beyond destitution and alienation to make delectable food. You have only to taste a culturally new dish, such as the *enchiladas de queso* (recipe page 40), to understand how something new and beautiful is created out of brokenness and change. In the recipe, you will see that the dish combines and contrasts the tangy, tart European milk product with the complex depth of selected indigenous chiles.

Two interesting dynamics of ancient times, continuing up to the 1500s and into the twentieth century influenced the distinctive style of cooking that evolved into today's Texas Mexican cuisine.

Exchange within the Triangle and into Northeastern Mexico

Trade and reciprocity agreements fostered an ongoing exchange of ideas, tools, methods, and products among the distinct peoples of this Texas Mexican triangle. Through a system of trails and riverways, they carried on not only trade with each other, but also violent raids into each other's territory for certain goods. They customarily married into other's tribes to avoid the taboo of incest.

These types of exchange and marriage practices extended seamlessly south into northeastern Mexico, which has climatic and geographic conditions similar to south Texas. Included are the present Mexican states of Tamaulipas, Nuevo León, northern San Luis Potosí, northeastern Zacatecas, and northeastern Coahuila. In the 1800s Comanches were raiding for livestock hundreds of miles into Mexico. This larger area, a region of about two hundred miles on either side of the lower Rio Grande, was called by earlier scholars the Coahuiltecan region, taking the name from the Mexican state of Coahuila.

Chroniclers of the sixteenth and seventeenth centuries grouped together the many distinct native tribes or bands of this region on both sides of the river as a single people, thinking that they all spoke the same language, Coahuiltecan. But now scholars believe that the more than a thousand bands spoke a variety of languages. They did share some cooking habits and technologies such as baking in earthen ovens, drying, roasting, grinding, boiling, and steaming. But the extent to which they had the same culture declines in the face of new studies showing that the various bands were in fact autonomous and had different cultural practices, such as in types of garments and food collection. In order to recognize the similarities of the bands in this region while acknowledging that they cannot be considered as a single cultural group, David La Vere says that it is probably more accurate to see the communities as "a wide scattering of bands with a similar hunter-gatherer economy adapted to the arid country of southern Texas and northeastern Mexico" (La Vere, 2004, p. 65).

Bordering just above the triangle lived the Tonkawas, and along the coast the Karankawas. I include them as major groups in the development of our cuisine because exchange in the region among these peoples and with those in the triangle was constant.

Exchange through Trade Routes into Mesoamerica

Trade and communication with northern Mexico and the Valley of Mexico were ongoing via roads and river routes, and thus with Mesoamerican cultures and the Aztec, Toltec, and Teotihuacán civilizations. This presents an even larger region with which the Texas Indians communicated and traded. In northern Mexico, the Rio Conchos comes up from the Sierra Madre Occidental deep in southwest Chihuahua, and travels northward to meet the Rio Grande at Ojinaga, halfway between El Paso and Del Rio.

The Camino Real road system that the Spaniards used as they traveled to Texas from Mexico City in the late seventeenth century consisted of routes originally created by indigenous people. One such *camino* came up from Zacatecas, passed through Saltillo and Monclova, crossed the Rio Grande just forty-seven miles south of my childhood home in Nava, Coahuila, and went on to San Antonio, my other childhood town, and eastward from there (McGraw, 2003). Mexican pottery and other cooking utensils were traded through these indigenous routes. Ideas, ingredients, and surely even recipes were shared.

The Spanish, of course, used these routes to govern and connect Mexico City with various government centers and missions. These connections preceded the Spanish conquest and hence there was a degree of homogeneity in the various cuisines of this larger Mexico region. Oaxaca Mexican cuisine is similar to but also differs from Puebla Mexican and Sonora Mexican cuisine. Likewise these three are similar to but also differ from Texas Mexican cuisine.

The Spanish Camino Real consisted of routes created originally by indigenous people. This route, from Zacatecas, passed through Saltillo and Monclova, crossed the Rio Grande just 47 miles south of my childhood town, Nava, Coahuila, and went on to San Antonio. Reprinted with permission from *Texas Almanac*, Texas State Historical Association, http://www.TexasAlmanac.com.

The following descriptions include aspects of life and cooking dating back far before the arrival of Europeans, knowledge that we have today thanks to archaeological explorations. I also include aspects of life after 1500, which is when Europeans began to write about the Texas Indians in their journals. The picture of Texas Indian life before and after 1500 is one of family and community. Survival certainly, but like all of us, the people were just attending to what each day brings: ups and downs of human life—grief, friendships, farewells, celebrations—and all the while gathering food and cooking.

Women's roles included gathering food, child rearing, planting, and cooking. They made their mark on and sustained the tribal survival economy. Although often in secondary roles to male authority, they carried the day at times of important decision making such as making war, choosing a partner, or staying married (Newcomb, 1961). The Indian view was that women held up half the sky. The roles of men were those of warrior, trader, hunter, and fisherman. Men were competitive and held wrestling matches and races with one another. Both men and women adhered to a religious or spiritual worldview. Religion was less a proscriptive set of rules and more an ethical understanding of the world as a spiritual context, with dreams having great significance and spirit powers dwelling everywhere on the land. Harmony and balance were central.

The area that is home to Texas Mexican cuisine has three different geographic and climatic regions that provided the resources our ancestors used for cooking. They are the central, coastal, and south Texas regions.

Central

Situated above San Antonio, roughly from Boerne to Brenham and as far north as Waco, this land was home to the Tonkawa people who eventually shared land with Apaches, Kiowa, and Comanches. Some historians describe the Tonkawas as an amalgam of many different groups that because of necessity organized themselves to become the Tonkawa in the seventeenth century (La Vere, 2004).

They were a matrilineal society, meaning that after marriage the husband and the children belonged to the family line of the mother. The women gathered food and cooked it. Men were constantly on the hunt for food using bows and arrows and spears (Tonkawa Tribe of Oklahoma, 2012). They hunted deer that the women prepared in a variety of ways including boiling, roasting, and also drying, as in deer jerky. They also hunted rabbits, skunks, rats, land tortoises, and rattlesnakes (considered a delicacy). Cooks used clay pots, since they were pottery makers. They traded and obtained more elaborate pottery and other products from the Caddos, their easternmost Texas neighbors who were excellent farmers and pottery makers. The Caddos made a corn stew called *sagamite*, which they cooked in their clay pots and served at gatherings with elders and chiefs (Wilson, 2012).

Cooks used chiles (Dial and Black, 2010) and combined seasonings with meat, as they did, for example, with a dish called pemmican, deer meat that was dried, pounded, combined with pecan meal, and stuffed into casings like sausage. Between 1200 and 1500, buffalo migrated across the southern plains and provided an additional food source (Anderson, 1999). Coyotes and wolves were not eaten for religious reasons (Newcomb, 1961). Tonkawas dug up wild onions, picked wild hackberry from bushes, nuts from the little walnut trees, and ate the roots, leaves, or flowers of yucca, sotol, and *lechugilla* (variety of agave) plants. Roasting the underground bulbs such as sotol would take two days,

23

after which they would grind them and make them into cakes, perhaps with the addition of berries or savory wild onion. Just north of Fredericksburg, archaeologists have discovered granite bedrock mortars used for grinding and mashing that go back thousands of years (Potter, n.d.). I surmise that perhaps they might have also added a little liquid to the mortar and made a purée. Though mainly hunter gatherers, they did at times cultivate small patches of corn (La Vere, 2004).

The rivers provided freshwater clams, blue catfish, river carp sucker, smallmouth buffalo fish, flathead catfish, and channel or blue catfish. There is also evidence that small, minnow-sized fish were part of the diet. And some anthropologists have found that snails were also eaten, since they were found in abundance in an excavated cooking hearth above San Marcos. All were mature adults so it is not likely that they were simply a colony of snails, as that would have included snails at various stages of maturation (Dial and Black, 2005).

As happened to all the Indian people of Texas, the Tonkawas eventually faced two choices regarding their homeland: leave or die. European diseases accounted for incalculable numbers of deaths as did fighting with other Indians, Europeans, Mexicans, and eventually Texans. Policies of ethnic cleansing won the day. By the 1830s, 1840s, and 1850s, Indian removal became a central theme of Texas history (Anderson, 2005). Many Tonkawas fled to Mexico, others married into tribes toward the east, and still others took refuge in Catholic missions and became workers, and thus in time part of the Mexican *campesinos* (agricultural workers). Those who remained as Tonkawa were forcibly removed to Oklahoma in 1885. In June every year now, the Tonkawa commemorate their forced relocation out of Texas and into Oklahoma, referred to as their own Trail of Tears. According to their online statement, the commemoration takes place "lest we forget" (Tonkawa Tribe of Oklahoma, n.d.).

Coastal

Beautiful, awesome, and dramatic are the words that come to mind about the Texas Gulf Coast. Again in the back of the pickup truck, we would drive through Sinton toward Corpus Christi, filled with anticipation and already smelling the salt air. We would romp on the beach and fish for redfish, drum, and now and then my older cousins would lunge out of the water with a large gleaming conch in their hands, a prize catch.

The Karankawas, standing six feet tall, inhabited the coast for thousands of years. They were comprised of many small groups along the coast. The Cocos in Galveston were the northernmost group. The Cujanes, Carancaguases, Coapites, and Copanes each inhabited a separate part of the coast all the way down to Corpus Christi. Little is known about the people who lived in the coastal area south of Corpus Christi but they are not grouped with the Karankawa. One group known as Borrados inhabited the coast south of Corpus Christi to Brownsville.

The Karankawa were patrilineal and had strict rules regarding social relationships within their community and with in-laws. Being hunters and gatherers, they fashioned canoes from tree trunks to navigate the shallow estuaries and bays where during the fall and winter months they harvested clams, blue crabs, oysters, and scallops, as well as conches in tide passes closer to the gulf. They roasted these foods on rocks or shells or steamed them in shell-lined hearths (Dial and Black, 2009). Shellfish, being small and providing small quantities of food, needed to be harvested in large amounts. In the freshwater streams and rivers they caught catfish, redfish or red drum, black drum, and Atlantic croaker. They used harpoons, bows and arrows, baited shell hooks, and also nets that they made from the fiber of nearby fibrous plants. They smoked or dried the fish and I can just imagine one or other cook adding some crushed pecans or other ingredients to enhance the flavor. I can never know for sure but how different could they have been from me as a cook?

The Karankawa cook had these additional local resources: tortoise, frogs, and the very-difficult-to-catch alligator. Alligator grease was also applied all over the body to repel mosquitos. Now that is a mosquito repellent you don't see advertised on TV. They hunted mallard ducks and other water fowl, including the whooping crane, which is now endangered.

At the change of seasons in the spring and summer months, the Karankawas moved as much as twenty-five miles inland to hunt deer, rabbits, raccoons, opossums, javelinas, and turkeys (Kenmotsu and Dial, 2009). Unlike the Tonkawas, the Karankawas did hunt and eat foxes and coyotes. They also gathered roots, fruits, and nuts. Although there is no evidence about specific roots used, some of the roots found in this area are arrowhead root, cattail or tule, and a flower with edible corms known as spring beauty. The Karankawas were pottery makers so they used wide-mouthed jars resting on coals to cook and serve. And to my delight,

one of their culinary dishes was a delectable corn cake that they made with ground corn and then baked on simmering ashes. That sounds delicious. To this day many Texans sing the praises of the wonderful smoke taste in their cornbread when they cook it outdoors in a smoke pit or hearth (Gatschet, Hammond, and Oliver, 1891). I wonder if sometimes the Karankawas added cut-up spring beauty corms to the cakes before baking. I would have.

The Karankawa homeland, language, and cultural identity suffered a violent and bitter demise beginning in 1528 at the moment they found four bedraggled, starving strangers on their coast, today's Galveston Island: the conquest-bound Spaniard, Cabeza de Vaca, his two companions and their African slave (Cabeza de Vaca, 2003). The Karankawa nursed the four back to health and incorporated them into their group, assigning them the many daily menial tasks necessary for group survival. Cabeza de Vaca's journal provides much of the information that we have about the cultures and practices of Texas Indians.

By the early 1800s, the Karankawas had been devastated by Spanish diseases and were continually struggling to repel raids and attacks from Comanches, Apaches, and Tonkawas. Republic of Texas settlers posed the final threat. In 1824 Stephen F. Austin, convinced that the Karankawas had to be exterminated, led an expedition of ninety men against the Karankawas who then took refuge at La Bahía mission. Enmities and violence continued until 1858 when a number of Texans led by Juan Nepomuceno Cortina attacked the few remaining Karankawa living near Rio Grande City and killed them (Lipscomb, 2012).

Southern

This area extends from San Antonio all the way south to the Rio Grande. I lived one glorious year in Sarita, off Baffin Bay and south of Corpus Christi, and from there I drove to many of the unhurried small towns mainly in the south of this expansive semi-desert. It feels hot, and when standing in the completely flat chaparral brushlands, the sky seems enormous. The main metropolitan area in the southernmost tip, the Rio Grande valley of Texas, is comprised of three major cities—McAllen, Edinburgh, and Mission. The 2010 Census found it to have the highest poverty rate of any metropolitan area its size or larger (Crandall, 2012). Mexican Americans comprise nearly 90 percent of the population of the Rio Grande valley (Starchannel Communications, n.d.). It is likely that most, or even all, are descendants of Texas Indians.

Following is a sample of the recorded names of more than three hundred distinct groups who lived in this southern Texas region for more than ten thousand years: Aguapalam, Aguastaya, Anxau Apaysi, Archjomo, Ataxal, Cachopostal, Cauya, Chayopin, Geyer Juanca, Manico Mescal, Ocana Paac, Paachiqui, Pacao Pachal, Pachaque, Pacoa Pacpul, Pacuache, Pajalat, Pamaya, Pampopa, Papanac, Pastaloca, Pastia Patacal, Pataguo, Patumaco, Patzau, Pausane, Payaya, Payuguan, Pitahay, Pitalac, Pulacuam, Quem, Sacuache, Samampac, Sampanal, Sanaque, Saracuam, Semonan, Siaguam, Siquipil, Sonayan, Sulujam, Tacame Tilijae, Tilpacopal, Tepacuache, and Yorica (Kenmotsu, Dial, and Black, 2006). As mentioned earlier, the name Coahuiltecan was mistakenly applied to all groups in the region, extending down into Mexico, upon making the assumption that all comprised a single cultural and linguistic group. This is not the case and so the name should apply only to the general geographic area and not to the culturally disinct peoples living there.

Unlike the Tonkawas, these groups were patrilineal, with women and children becoming part of the man's family group. Mainly comprised of a large extended family, they had shamans who acted as doctors and dealt with the spirit world, performing rites at religious ceremonies and dances. As with the Tonkawas and the Karankawas, the women cared for the children, gathered food, and cooked, while the men hunted and went on war raids. Also as among the Tonkawas and Karankawas, there was a third gender role, the homosexual. Some women took on roles and acted like men. Some men dressed as women and lived as they did, doing the same work of gathering and cooking. Homosexual men accompanied Indian warriors when they went to war, since women could not go (Foster, 1995). As a third way of sexuality, they were thought to possess special spiritual powers and participated in religious ceremonies (La Vere, 2004).

The people of the Coahuiltecan region did not generally plant gardens so all the vegetables and roots they ate had to be gathered. These included mesquite beans, pecans, prickly pear cactus, sotol, lechugilla, maguey, wild onion, a host of berries and fruit, such as condalia, persimmon, and agarito, and likely amaranth, chiles, and herbs such as Mexican oregano (Dial and Black, 2010). One of the soups they made was a mesquite cold soup or drink. Mesquite bean pods were gathered and placed inside a hole they had dug in the ground. The pods were pounded with a large wooden log as thick as a man's leg until the mesquite was a fine powder. Earth was added to sweeten it, and then the powder was ground again. They then placed the powder in a vessel that was a two-handled basket, and after adding water, drank it (Cabeza de Vaca, 2003). I'll have to try this at my next dinner party.

Nuts could be roasted but plant roots had to be cooked for two days in dug-out earth ovens. Pounding or grinding ingredients to make powders and flours and to blend several flavors was a much used culinary technique. The process produced a culinary product that the Spaniards called *mesquitamal*. It was a flour that the women made by grinding mesquite beans and combining them with pulverized dried berries, seeds, and other ingredients. As far south as Monclova, one hundred miles from my hometown of Nava, Coahuila, Cabeza de Vaca describes another pounded dish, green pine nuts ground up and formed into little nuggets that were eaten raw (Cabeza De Vaca, 2003). In many ways, our ancestors shared an affinity with my friends today who are raw-food vegans.

Using bows and arrows, the men hunted deer, pronghorn, rabbits, raccoons, opossums, javelinas, badgers, shrews, moles, skunks, and even bison. Around 1500, bison traveled as far south as southern Texas and northern Mexico, but as mentioned earlier, the spreading of mesquite eventually prevented bison from migrating that far south (Anderson, 1999). Birds included turkeys and roadrunners as well as various ducks and geese. Bird eggs were also gathered for food (Dial, 2006). Oftentimes I wish one of the chroniclers of the 1500s and 1600s had been a culinarian. He or she then might have described, for example, how they cooked those bird eggs. In today's Texas Mexican cuisine we boil and fry chicken eggs. We also use eggs to make batters for frying vegetables and seafood.

Fish included catfish, gar, and freshwater drum, which were shot with a bow and arrow or caught using a hook made of bone. At night they would hunt with torches that would attract the fish (Newcomb, 1961). They roasted their catch on an open fire. Great culinary customs never die, for today we delight in the same open-fire fish preparation, taking in the aroma and admiring the clouds during the day and at night the brilliant stars.

The custom of eating snails is also one we share with the Indians of south Texas. Snails could be found beneath rocks and logs and on low branches. Pop one in your mouth for a quick snack. In streams and rivers they also caught freshwater clams that were eaten steamed or raw (Dial and Black, 2010).

The same story repeated itself here. They came under attack from the Apaches from the north as well as the Comanches, adding to the destruction caused by intertribal conflicts. Anglo Texan encroachments and U.S. expansion combined to make Texas during this time a horrible place of chaos and violence. The south Texas peoples were hit from all sides. They suffered the rampant diseases, such as measles, smallpox, and cholera brought by Europeans. It was especially terrible because oral cultures need time to pass on knowledge about medicine, botany, history, philosophy, and culinary arts. Time ran out. They dispersed. Some fled or were taken captive into Mexico. Others chose the temporary safety of the Catholic missions. Over time all who survived blended and became the Mexican people (Kenmotsu, Dial, and Black, 2006).

27

PART II:
RECIPES

3

TOOLS AND INGREDIENTS

Described here are items that appear repeatedly in the recipes in this book. They are staples in my kitchen and you might find making them part of your kitchen enjoyable and useful.

Comal

A *comal* is an iron griddle used for roasting, browning, and heating. Mine is an 8-inch by 12-1/2-inch, cast-iron rectangle with a handle. I can cook two corn tortillas at a time. My father made it for me using a welding torch. It is a gift that I treasure.

Cast iron *comal* (griddle).

Bean Masher

Also called a potato masher, this metal tool is for mashing beans in a frying pan after they have been cooked and are soft. Like the one my mom used, mine has a rectangular base, 4-1/4 inches by 3 inches, and formed by tines winding back and forth, zig-zag fashion, and a 10-inch-long handle. What makes this tool preferable to a blender is that you can control the degree of mashing, giving texture to the bean dish by leaving some bits whole.

Dried Chiles

Dried chiles reflect the creativity and ingenuity of cooks. Not only does drying preserve the chiles but it can also accentuate or enrich flavors. All of the following chiles are purchased dry.

Chile ancho is a dried ripe *poblano* chile.
Chile chipotle is a dried, ripe jalapeño chile that has been smoked over a wood fire.
Chile guajillo is a dried *mirasol* chile.
Chile mulato is the dried version of the chile by the same name, *mulato*. It is very similar to the chile ancho (dried ripe poblano) but has a browner color and a richer taste.
Chile pasilla is a dried, ripe *chilaca* chile.

Metal Tortilla Press

My mother never used this tool because she made corn tortillas by hand, slapping a small ball of *masa* back and forth between her outstretched hands. The ball of masa became thinner and larger as it whirled and morphed into a perfectly round tortilla, ready to go onto the hot *comal* that sizzled as the tortilla was released. *Amá* did this so effortlessly that it seemed the tortillas shaped themselves. Keeping a bowl of water near, she kept her hands always moist and whenever little bits of masa broke off the swirling tortilla, her fingers would deftly paste another bit back on. *Amá* making corn tortillas is a movie that runs in my mind all the time: slap, slap, slap, paste a little masa back on, slap, slap, slap, onto the comal, sizzle.

I am still trying to perfect the technique and, in the meantime employ a metal round tortilla press that is sold online and in most grocery stores in our barrios. It is simply two round disks that fold, one on top of the other, and are pressed together by a lever. The more pressure you apply, the thinner the tortilla. Mine is small, 6-1/2 inches in diameter.

Molcajete and Tejolote

The *molcajete* is a volcanic rock bowl, a mortar that rests on three short legs. I use it every day to grind spices, make chile pastes, salsas, and guacamoles. I use it because it grinds things to a very fine powder or paste, much finer than you can get from a blender or a spice grinder. Mine is 8 inches in diameter, and the three little legs are barely 1 inch high so it will not topple over when you work with it. I think this is the perfect size for most kitchens. Molcajetes are passed from one generation to the next. I have a smaller one that my mother used and gave to me. I will never get rid of it, and one day my two molcajetes will be passed on to a niece or nephew.

The pestle is named *tejolote*, also made of volcanic

rock. Mine is cone shaped and 4 inches in length, top to bottom. It works so efficiently that I can grind a sliced chile serrano into a fine paste in only five seconds—honestly.

To clean the *molcajete* and *tejolote*, just give them a quick rinse with water and a brush. Do not use soap.

To prepare them for use when newly purchased, put two tablespoons of white rice in the *molcajete* and grind vigorously with the *tejolote*. The rice will turn gray as

Molcajete and *tejolote*.

the volcanic rock is ground with it. Throw away the rice and repeat this process until the white rice that you grind is completely white, with no more volcanic dust.

I think you will enjoy using this ancient tool in your kitchen. Mesoamericans started using it thousands of years ago. Here in Texas our ancestors used mortars made of granite (Potter, n.d.). There is ample archaeological evidence that prehistoric Mesoamericans used the *molcajete*, made from volcanic rock, in central and southern Mexico (De Gortari, 1961). Near Victoria, Texas, there is evidence of Mexican-style ceramic *molcajetes* dating to the 1700s (Dockall and Black, 2007).

Palote

The *palote* is a rolling pin used to roll wheat flour tortillas. As I grew up it was always in our family's kitchen and now it is always in mine. My palote is 14 inches long with a diameter of 1-1/2 inches. I went to the local hardware store's lumber section where they sell wooden dowels, and sawed off a 14-inch piece. It cost $1.29.

Mexican Oreganos

When I indicate Mexican oregano in the ingredients section of the recipes, I mean *Poliomintha longiflora*. Oregano is an essential part of the Texas Mexican flavor profile and so it is important to distinguish between two different herbs called Mexican oregano.

Poliomintha longiflora is naturalized in Texas and in the Mexican northern states of Nuevo León, Coahuila, and San Luis Potosí (Sánchez, Medellín, and Aldama, 2007). It likes the heat. It blooms spectacularly with clusters of tiny pink or lavender bell-shaped flowers. A member of the mint herb family, it is delicious in all my recipes. It grows free and healthy in my garden and I hope you will consider planting one in your garden or in a pot.

The other herb that is called Mexican oregano, *Lippia graveolens* is a member of the verbena herb family. It is the default oregano herb for most central and southern Mexico cuisine dishes (Meléndez Rentería, Rodríguez Herrera, Silva Vázquez, and Nevárez Moorillon, 2009), and we sometimes use it in Texas Mexican cuisine because it is more readily available in stores. It is aromatic and delicious.

Piloncillo

In the recipes I recommend use of *piloncillo* rather than brown sugar. Piloncillo is unrefined cane syrup that is boiled down and put into molds that are most often conic in shape. The flavor is natural and complex.

Yerbaniz or Pericón

Native to Mexico and Guatemala where it is used to prepare corn and chayote dishes, this hardy, sun-loving herb also has ritualistic and spiritual uses (Universidad Autónoma del Estado de México, 2010). It is naturalized all over south Texas and in my garden. Growing up, we drank it as a tea, a remedy for colds and stomach aches. I include it here in some of my new recipes to point to its many culinary uses, some of which are being discovered by talented chefs today. In Mexico it is called *pericón* and *yerbaniz*. In the United States it has many aliases, including Texas tarragon, Mexican tarragon, Mexican mint marigold, and sweet mace. Scientists named it *Tagetes lucida*. We call it "yerbaniz."

Texas Mexican oregano *(Poliomintha longiflora)*.

34

Yerbaniz (Tagetes lucida) is also called *pericón* in Spanish. In English, its aliases include Mexican tarragon, Mexican mint marigold, and sweet mace.

Cazuelitas.

4

CORN AND BEANS

Cazuelitas or Sopes

(makes 18–20 cazuelitas)

A dish that we have in common with other regions but with delightful variations is the *sope* or *cazuelita* (little casserole). It is made of corn and stuffed with an assortment of fillings. In Mexico City *sopes* are like *gorditas* with a rim around them, but fried. And in Oaxaca a similar dish, *memelas*, is oblong, flatter, and also fried. Our Texas dish is sometimes called *sopes* and other times *cazuelitas*. It is changing in interesting ways, and this recipe is one that is baked rather than fried, thus dramatically lowering the amount of fat. A dish with no lard and reduced fat is traditional.

Ingredients

    1 pound corn flour
    3/4 cup canola oil
    2-1/2 cups water
    1 teaspoon salt

Method

1. Combine the corn flour, oil, water, and salt to make *masa*. The masa should feel like very pliable and moist clay. If you need a little more water, add 1 or 2 tablespoons at a time.

2. Cover the *masa* with a damp cloth and let it rest for 20–30 minutes to absorb moisture.
3. Preheat oven to 375°F.
4. Roll 18–20 small masa balls with your hands and press them into little 1/4-inch thick tortillas either with your hands or a tortilla press. Keep them covered with a damp towel.
5. With your fingers make a high rim all around, fashioning what look like little cooking pots or casseroles (cazuelitas).
6. Place in the preheated oven on an ungreased baking sheet and bake for 20–30 minutes.

After they are baked and golden, fill them with *picadillo*, *chorizo con papas*, or guacamole. They can be served hot or at room temperature.

Chalupas or Tostadas

(serves 6)

Chalupas take me back to first grade when volunteer ladies from the neighborhood would come to the school kitchen and make these as snacks for us in the middle of the afternoon. A culinary playground.

Chalupas are made even more delicious when you can build them yourself, satisfying your taste urges and personal preferences. You deserve to get what you want, so interact with the ingredients, live it up. Refried beans always form the bottom layer of the chalupa. My sister, Fina, reminded me that for her, the best way is to not put anything at all on top but enjoy only the deliciously fresh corn tortillas adorned with perfectly cooked beans, *frijoles refritos*. I agree with her. My second favorite is to top with shredded iceberg lettuce, tomato, and onion. No cheese, thank you.

But this is a party recipe, so you can pile on anything you want, celebrating historically tested flavors, and exploring new ones. Make an array of contrasting and complementary toppings to suit your party.

Ingredients

12 corn tortillas
1/4 cup vegetable oil
2 ripe tomatoes, small dice
2 cups finely sliced iceberg lettuce
1/2 cup white onion, small dice
3 cups frijoles refritos (well-fried beans; recipe on page 45)

Method

1. Preheat oven to 350°F.
2. On cookie sheets, very lightly brush both sides of the tortillas with the vegetable oil and bake for 15–20 minutes or until the color of the tortillas turns a deep tan. If the tortillas are too light, they haven't cooked long enough and will be chewy rather than crisp.
3. When they are done, stack the crisp tortillas on a large platter, ready for the guests.
4. Place the tomato, onion, and lettuce in separate bowls so that guests can layer them on the chalupas.
5. Keep the beans warm on the stove, or in a crockpot or chafing dish.

You can add the following ingredients to the table: guacamole, various salsas, *chorizo* (see recipe on page 83), and *carnitas* (see recipe on page 104).

38

Chalupas or *tostadas*.

Cornbread Dressing

(makes 1-1/2 quarts)

Ingredients

3 cups cornbread (from page 51)
3/4 cup white onion, small dice
1/3 cup celery, small dice
1/2 cup green *chile dulce* (bell pepper), small dice
2 tablespoons canola oil or other vegetable oil
1/2 cup pecan pieces, roasted on a cookie sheet in a 350°F oven for 8 minutes (Be careful not to burn them.)
1/4 cup black raisins
3/4 cup beef stock or broth
1/4 teaspoon salt

Method

1. Heat oven to 350°F.
2. Make cornbread (see page 51) and after it cools, slice a portion that will measure 3 cups when crumbled. Use your fingers or a food processor to crumble the bread. Crumbs should be no larger than the size of a pea. Set aside in a large bowl.
3. In a skillet, heat the oil on medium heat and add the onion, celery, and chile dulce. Cook while stirring until the vegetables are soft, about 4 minutes.
4. Add the cooked vegetables to the cornbread, along with the roasted pecans, raisins, and salt. Mix thoroughly.
5. Add the beef broth to the mixture and mix well with a large spoon or spatula. On Thanksgiving Day, my *amá* would use turkey broth instead of beef.
6. Place the ingredients in a casserole dish, cover and bake at 350°F for 30 minutes or until the dressing is heated through.

Enchiladas de Queso | Cheese Enchiladas

(serves 6)

Enchiladas marked special occasions in our home. To understand them is to understand our community. We could not normally afford cheese, but when we did, the cheese of choice was *queso fresco*, a fresh, mild-tasting, crumbly Mexican cheese. The industrial revolution had spawned Kraft's processed yellow cheese earlier, in the 1920s, and over time the processed yellow cheeses entered our Texas Mexican kitchens and changed the flavors. Whichever cheese you use, just make sure that it has a mild, unobtrusive flavor and the least possible fat. After all, chiles play the primary role in this dish. That is why it is called "enchiladas."

I'm glad to share this recipe because it is quintessentially Texas Mexican.

1. **It grounds us in our region.** The discriminating blending of different types of chiles links us to the other communities in our geographic region who also combined chiles in different variations to make different dishes. Think Guanajuato, Puebla, Oaxaca, and so on.
2. **It integrates Texas Indian with European ingredients.** Actually its success as a culinary dish results exactly from the successful integration of native with foreign ingredients—beautiful culinary marriages, in this case, chiles with wheat flour and

Enchiladas de queso.

Mexican oregano with cumin. The same happened in Oaxaca with *mole*, using wheat bread as a thickener for chiles.

Ingredients

4 ancho chiles, seeded and deveined
1 pasilla chile, seeded and deveined
1/4 teaspoon cumin powder
2 garlic cloves
1/8 teaspoon black peppercorns
1 teaspoon salt
2-inch sprig of Texas Mexican oregano
1/4 cup all-purpose wheat flour
2 tablespoons canola oil
8 cups water
18 corn tortillas
1 white onion, finely diced
2 cups queso fresco, crumbled

Method

For the Chile Paste

1. To devein the chiles, first lay the chile flat on a cutting board and, using a paring knife, cut a slit lengthwise. Grab the chile with one hand and with the other remove the stem along with the bunch of seeds still attached to it. Open the chile along the slit and take out the remaining seeds and veins.

2. In a large saucepan, cover the cleaned chiles with water and bring to a boil. Turn off the heat and let the chiles steep for 15 minutes so that they rehydrate and become tender.

3. Drain the chiles, discarding the water. Let the chiles cool a bit so as not to damage your blender. Then place the chiles in a blender along with the cumin, garlic, black peppercorns, salt, and oregano. Add 1/2–1 cup clean water and blend to a very fine paste. If there are any small flecks, strain through a fine-mesh sieve.

This chile–spice combination is the focal point. It is what you want to taste first and throughout. All the other elements of the dish play supporting and contrasting roles.

4. Finely dice the onion and set aside. Crumble the *queso fresco* and also set aside. My sister, Nieves Ortega, reminded me about how important it is that the onion dice be tiny. It allows the onion and the chiles to blend evenly. If the onion pieces are too large, you get too much onion acid when you chew. Onions are a naturally delicious combination with chile and you want your mouth to easily blend and taste chile–onion as a principal "yum."

5. In a saucepan or large skillet, heat the oil over medium heat and add the chile paste. Take precautions against splatter. Cook for about 4–5 minutes until you see the color deepen a bit.

6. Dissolve the flour completely in the 8 cups of water. Add it to the chile and bring to a rolling boil. Continue boiling for about 30 minutes until the flour has cooked completely, the chile thickens, and the flavors develop. You should have about 3–4 cups. Taste and adjust the salt.

7. While keeping the chile hot over medium heat, use two tongs or spatulas to immerse a corn tortilla in the hot chile for about 8–12 seconds until it is heated through and soft but holding its structure. If

heated too long, it will fall apart. If heated for too short a time it will not soften properly. After a few times you will get the feel of it.

8. Place the chile-infused tortilla flat on a warm platter and add 2 tablespoons cheese and 1/2 tablespoon diced onions. Roll them and arrange seam down on each plate. Repeat with all the tortillas, three per plate.

9. Spoon 1/3 cup of the steaming chile onto each plate and garnish with additional diced onions and cheese.

I hope you will experience nuanced taste. The chile carries the dish, and the various ingredients provide differences in textures and aromas, both individually and together. I think it is a special pleasure to enjoy food and understand the link to the people who created it.

Frijoles Borrachos, Frijoles Charros | Drunken Beans, Charro Beans

Recipe (serves a party of 8–10)

Ingredients

1 pound pinto beans, picked over for debris and rinsed

3 slices bacon, cut into 1-inch pieces

1 cup beer (if you omit the beer, you will have frijoles charros)

2 tablespoons salt

1 cup white onion, small dice

4 coarsely diced small tomatoes (about 4 cups)

1-1/2 tablespoons finely diced chile serrano

(remove seeds if you want a less hot, or *menos picante*, version)

1 bunch cilantro, coarsely chopped

Frijoles borrachos, frijoles charros.

Method

1. Pick through the beans to remove any little rocks or debris, rinse them, and then place them in a large pot and cover them with water rising 3 inches above the beans. Add the beer, bacon, and salt and bring to a boil. Turn down the heat to a slow simmer and cook for about 2–4 hours until they are completely soft. Add more water during the cooking as needed so that they do not dry out. I place them in a crockpot, medium or high setting, and cook for 6–8 hours.

2. When the beans are cooked, add the onion, tomato, and the chile and cook for 20 minutes. Just before serving, add the bunch of coarsely chopped cilantro. My sister, Esther, who taught me this recipe, cautions anyone who makes it to avoid overcooking the onion and tomato.

Serve in small bowls and just watch the smiles on everyone's faces.

Frijoles con Chorizo | Beans with Mexican Chorizo

(serves 8–10 as an appetizer)

Serve as a bean dip with corn tortilla chips, garnished with *jalapeños en escabeche* (pickled).

Ingredients

  2 cups pinto beans (12 ounces by weight)
  1-1/2 cup chorizo (from the store or the recipe on page 83)
  1/4 cup white onion, diced
  2 tablespoons canola or vegetable oil
  1/8 teaspoon salt

Method

1. Pick through the beans to remove any little rocks or debris, and then rinse them in a colander. If you have time, place the beans in a container, cover them with water, and let them soak overnight. Then drain them and discard the water. At this point, the beans will be ready to cook and take less time than unsoaked beans. I never soak them, nor did my mom.

2. To cook the beans, place them in a pot and add the salt and enough water to rise 3 inches above the beans. Bring to a slow simmer and cook on low heat, covered, for 4 hours, or 1-1/2 hours if they have been soaked. To test for doneness, press one bean between your thumb and forefinger. It should be completely soft and offer no resistance.

3. Mash the beans with a bean masher or in a blender. Set aside.

4. Heat the oil in a skillet and cook the chorizo until it is slightly crispy, about 10 minutes.

5. Add the onions and cook for another 2 minutes.

6. Add the beans to the chorizo mixture and mix well. Adjust the salt.

These are also delicious as a topping for *cazuelitas* or *sopes* (page 37) finished off with a sprinkle of *queso fresco*.

Frijoles de Olla con Cebolla | Clay Pot Beans with Onion

(serves 8)

Sometimes in mid-afternoon, we would have a bowl of these beans. The hot, steaming beans are contrasted with the acidic bite of onion.

Ingredients

2 cups pinto beans (12 ounces by weight)

6 cups water

1/4 white onion

1 garlic clove, peeled

1/2 teaspoon salt

1/2 white onion, small dice

Method

1. Pick through the beans to remove any debris, and then rinse them in a colander.
2. Place the water and beans in a large pot, and a clay pot if you have one, since it is the clay pot or *olla* for which this recipe is named. Add the garlic, 1/4 white onion, and salt.
3. Bring the water to a boil, turn down to a simmer and cook, covered, for 4 hours or until the beans are completely soft. Keep checking to make sure that the water rises at least 3 inches above the beans, adding additional water as needed.
4. Before serving, remove the onion and the garlic and adjust the salt. Serve the beans in small bowls, adding 1 tablespoon of diced onion.

Serve with hot corn tortillas.

Frijoles Refritos | Well-Fried Beans

(makes 6 cups of beans and broth)

I cringe when this dish is translated as refried beans because the unfortunate phrase leads some cooks to serve grease-and-beans. These beans are not twice fried, they are just properly fried. The prefix "re" in front of a Spanish word means properly done. I call "frijoles refritos" well-fried beans. I use only 1 table-spoon of canola oil. If you prefer to use lard instead of canola oil, the result will also be delicious.

Ingredients

3 cups dry pinto beans, picked over to remove debris and then washed

6 cups water

1/8 peeled white onion

1 peeled garlic clove

1/2 tablespoon salt

1 tablespoon canola oil

Method

1. Place all the ingredients except the oil in a crockpot and cook for 6 hours or until the beans are completely tender. I plug in the crockpot at night, set at medium or high, and go to sleep. The beans are done when they are completely soft, giving no resistance when you press them with your fingers.
2. Add the oil to a skillet on medium heat, along with 4 cups of beans, and an equal amount of water. Bring to a boil, and then lower the heat and, using a bean masher, mash the beans judiciously so that they are smooth but still have some texture.
3. Keep scraping the bottom of the skillet and brown the beans slowly for 30 minutes. This slow browning is what gives frijoles "refritos" their flavor, properly fried. I think it is reasonable to assume that our great great grandmothers were using this method, a type of roasting of the beans. It uses very little oil and lets the heat develop a rich, meaty flavor. At about 300°F the amino acids, or proteins, in the beans undergo a complex chemical change resulting in a transformation, a deepening, of the flavor.

45

Gorditas.

European scientists in the mid 1900s gave it the name, the Maillard reaction.

Serve at breakfast with scrambled eggs and flour tortillas, which was a common breakfast at our home. This dish makes a great scrambled eggs and bean taco, a traditional breakfast for us.

Gorditas

Recipe (makes 25 4-inch gorditas)

Ingredients

- 1 pound corn flour
- 2-1/2 cups water
- 2 teaspoons salt
- 1/2 cup canola oil

Method

1. Combine all the ingredients in a bowl to make a soft, moist *masa*. Add more water if needed, a tablespoon at a time. Cover with a damp cloth and let stand for 20 minutes.
2. Form the dough into 25 small balls, flatten them to 1/2 thickness. Keep them covered with a damp cloth.
3. Place the gorditas on a 375°F griddle or *comal*. After 2 minutes flip them and cook the other side also for 2 minutes. Now that both sides are nice and crunchy, just let each side cook for another 2–3 minutes until the gorditas are golden.

The inside will be buttery soft and the outside crunchy.

Gorditas con Queso Fresco

(makes 25 small gorditas)

Vary the size and you can have either finger food or a sit-down meal. You can develop tasty combinations of toppings, but I think the most successful ones are those based in history. Certain combinations of ingredients have been tested over centuries and my preference is to never change anything before I have understood the basic traditions.

Corn, or maize, was first domesticated in Mexico around 5000–7000 BCE (Gershenson, 2007). Nearer to us there is archaeological evidence of corn in a cave in New Mexico dated around 3500 BCE (Berzok, 2005). Corn arrived in Texas, in the northeast area, around 700 CE (La Vere, 2004) and ever since it has been central to our cuisine. All our neighbors make their own versions of gorditas. To the west in New Mexico, the Hopi and Pueblo recipes use rather slender tortillas flavored with guajillo chile. Down south, in Querétaro, Mexico, the corn *masa* is blended with ancho chile and cheese. The recipe I'm sharing is one that I have adapted from Texas and northeastern Mexico recipes that use *queso fresco*. I hope you find these gorditas as delicious as I do.

Ingredients

- 1 pound corn flour
- 2-1/2 cups water (If you need a little more, add 1–2 tablespoons at a time.)
- 6 ounces queso fresco, finely crumbled
- Salt to taste (I use 1/2 teaspoon.)
- 3 tablespoons canola oil or as needed to coat the *comal* or griddle

Method

1. Combine corn flour, salt, and water to make a *masa*.
2. Add the queso fresco and knead to combine thoroughly. The masa should feel like a soft, very pliable clay with no queso fresco lumps.
3. Cover the masa with a damp cloth and let rest for about 45 minutes.
4. Roll the masa into 25 balls, and then flatten each ball into a little 1/2-inch-thick gordita. Gordita means "little fat one." Have a bowl of water handy so that you can keep your hands slightly moist. This will keep the masa from sticking to your hands as you form the gorditas. Cover the gorditas with a damp cloth to keep them from drying.
5. Heat a cast-iron skillet or a griddle to 375°–400°F and apply a film of canola oil to the surface.
6. Place the gorditas on the griddle, cook for 2 minutes, and then flip and cook the other side also for 2 minutes. Now that both sides are crunchy, just let each side cook for another 2–3 minutes until the gorditas are deep golden.

   Split apart or slice with a knife or fork and fill with any of the following:

Layer of frijoles refritos topped with sliced iceberg lettuce, diced tomato, and onion

Spoonful of *chilorio* (pulled pork in chile; see recipe on page 107)

Guacamole

Various salsas

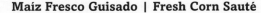

Maíz Fresco Guisado | Fresh Corn Sauté

Recipe (serves 4)

In Mexico, Aztec cultures affirm that our flesh and blood are made of corn (McKeever Furst, 2003). Many creation stories of native peoples in North America include corn as a central theme (Bastian and Mitchell, 2004). As a cook, I think corn is divine because it is delicious, versatile, and highly nutritious. We call it *elote*. When *amá* would make this *guisado*, or sautéed elote, for us, she would sit outdoors, peel off the shucks and, with a machete-like knife, slice away the kernels from the cob. She'd make a big batch for us. It was creamy and crunchy at the same time.

Ingredients

3 ears of fresh corn, washed, with kernels sliced off (2 cups)

1 tablespoon canola oil

1/4 teaspoon salt

1/2 cup water

Method

1. Heat a cast-iron skillet or other heavy skillet on high heat and add the canola oil.
2. When the oil is very hot and shimmering, add the fresh corn and spread it evenly across the skillet, allowing it to brown a bit. Add the salt and cook for 3 minutes, stirring occasionally. There will be some popping.
3. Add the water and deglaze the skillet. Heat until the water is almost completely evaporated but the corn is still moist.

That's it. Simplicity sometimes can be a revelation. *Buen provecho.*

Maíz fresco guisado.

Pan de maíz.

Pan de Maíz | Cornbread

Recipe (makes one 10-inch round)

This cornbread has a higher ratio of corn to wheat flour than Northern cornbread recipes and it is not sweet. It is typical of Texas Mexican versions, and of most U.S. Southern versions, which favor corn over wheat and also do not fiddle much with corn's natural sweetness. The small amount of sugar in this recipe helps maintain the moisture in the bread. I think you'll enjoy the extra crunch, especially the nice crust that forms by heating the cast-iron skillet before pouring in the batter. This crust is typical of almost all Southern-style cornbread recipes.

Ingredients

1 cup stone-ground cornmeal
3/4 cup all-purpose wheat flour
1/2 teaspoon baking soda
1-1/2 teaspoon baking powder
1/2 tablespoon sugar
1 teaspoon salt
2 tablespoons butter, melted
1 egg
1 egg white
1 cup buttermilk
1 tablespoon canola oil

Method

1. Preheat the oven to 425°F.
2. In a 10-inch, cast-iron skillet, add the canola oil and place in the oven to heat.
3. Sift together the wheat flour, soda, baking powder, sugar, and salt until thoroughly mixed.
4. Add the cornmeal and mix thoroughly.
5. In a separate bowl beat the egg and egg white.
6. Add the buttermilk and the melted butter to the beaten eggs and stir until fully combined.
7. Pour the egg and buttermilk mixture into the dry ingredients and stir gently with a large spoon, just enough to incorporate the liquid.
8. Remove the cast-iron skillet from the oven and pour the batter into it. Sizzle! Place in the oven and bake for about 25–30 minutes until golden brown.

Tamales de Frijol | Bean Tamales

(makes a dozen tamales, or a few more if you stretch the masa)

Traditional vegan dishes are an oft-overlooked dimension of Texas Mexican cuisine. These bean tamales are in every Mexican American home in Texas. Well, I cannot make such an absolute statement, but I can say that they were definitely in my home and in every home of my large extended family and neighbors. Even when we went to Nava, Coahuila, forty-five miles south of the Rio Grande, our relatives who lived there served tamales de frijol.

Bean tamales are also made in southern regions, such as in Puebla, Mexico. But they are slightly different and, of course, in Puebla they are served with *mole*, which is a truly wonderful combination. In most regions today, lard is used for the *masa*, but I use canola oil because of its low saturated fat content. It has a neutral taste that allows the flavors of the tamale filling

51

to come through. Yes, it is a return to the tamal that we used to make before the arrival of pigs, a kind of twist on the recent taste, and one that I like. My sister, Esther Martínez, taught me how to make tamales. This entire book would be less rich without her generous mentoring and instruction. She is a great cook, having learned important techniques from her mother-in-law, Antonia Martinez. Esther helped me get just the right texture of the *masa* and repeatedly told me that the fat has to be really hot when added to the masa. She guided me through many other recipes in this book.

We savor tamales on their own, just out of the husk, or sometimes with *salsa ranchera* if we really need some additional tang. Either way, your taste buds will have a holiday celebration.

Ingredients

For Masa and Husks

3-1/2 ounces dried corn husks (*hojas de maiz*), about 26 separate husks, soaked in hot water for at least 30 minutes

1 pound *masa* for tamales (This is a coarser grind than *masa* for tortillas, but not so coarse as cornmeal. It is called *masa quebrada*. In Houston, San Antonio, and most other Texas cities there are corn mills that make the freshly ground masa quebrada for tamales.)

1/2 cup canola oil

1/4–1/2 cup water if needed

For the Chile Paste

1 garlic clove

3 ancho chiles, cleaned, seeded, and deveined

3 guajillo chiles, cleaned, seeded, and deveined

1/2 teaspoon ground cumin

3/4 cup water

1 tablespoon canola oil

1 teaspoon salt or to taste

1/2–1 cup of water to blend the ingredients in a blender

For the Beans

1/2 pound beans (If you want to soak the beans overnight, they will cook more quickly, that is, in 1-1/2 hours. If you don't soak them [and I never do], cooking time will be 4 hours.)

1 teaspoon salt

5 cups water

Method

First, place the corn husks in a large container and cover them with hot water. Let them soak and soften for at least 30 minutes (or overnight if you like).

For the Chile Paste

1. To devein the chiles, first lay the chile flat on a cutting board and, using a paring knife, cut a slit lengthwise. Grab the chile with one hand and with the other remove the stem along with the bunch of seeds still attached to it. Open the chile along the slit and take out the remaining seeds and veins.

2. In a large saucepan, cover the cleaned chiles with water and bring to a boil. Turn off the heat and let the chiles steep for 15 minutes so that they rehydrate and become tender.

3. Drain the chiles, discarding the water. Let the chiles

cool a bit so as not to damage your blender, and then place the chiles in a blender along with the garlic, cumin, and salt. Blend to a very fine paste, adding about 1/2–1 cup water as needed.

4. In a Dutch oven, heat 1 tablespoon canola oil and fry the chile paste until it begins to change color and most of the liquid has evaporated. There will be splatter, so be prepared for it. Add 3/4 cup of water and simmer for about 15 minutes. The sauce will thicken and coat the back of a spoon.

For the Beans

5. Pick over the beans to remove any small stones or debris. Rinse them in a colander.

6. In a large pot, add the beans and salt. Cover the beans with 4 cups of water, bring to a boil, and then cover the pot and turn down the heat and simmer. As I mentioned above, if the beans have been soaked overnight you will cook them for 1-1/2 hours. If they have not been soaked, it will take 4 hours. As they cook, keep checking to make sure that you maintain the water level at least 3 inches above the beans, adding additional water as needed.

They are done when they give no resistance and are completely soft when you press one between your fingers. When the beans are completely cooked and soft, place a deep skillet on medium heat and add the beans and 2 cups of the bean liquid.

7. Using a bean masher, smash the beans until they are smooth and soupy, adding more liquid as needed. Alternately, you can use a blender to purée them before placing the beans in the skillet.

8. By this time, if you have made the chile paste, add 3 tablespoons chile paste to the beans and blend. If you don't have the paste made, just set the beans aside until you are ready to add the chile paste.

9. After adding the chile paste, cook on low heat, uncovered, until the mixture thickens into a thick, workable spread for the tamal filling.

For the Tamale Masa

10. In a stand mixer, using the paddle attachment, add 1/4 cup of the chile sauce to the masa and mix thoroughly.

11. In a saucepan, heat the oil just to the point where it begins to shimmer.

12. Adjust the mixer to low and carefully pour the hot oil (not warm but hot) into the *masa* to incorporate. It will sizzle as it makes contact, so watch out for splatter.

13. When the oil is incorporated, turn up the mixer to medium and mix well. Add water as needed to make a thick batter, which should be substantially thicker than pancake or cake batter but not so thick as the *masa* for tortillas.

14. Beginning 3 inches in from the pointed end of the husk, use a small spatula or spoon to spread 3 tablespoons *masa* on each corn husk.

15. Spoon about 1-1/2 tablespoons of the bean filling lengthwise on the masa, and then roll the husk lengthwise, firmly enveloping the filling.

16. Tightly fold the pointed tip toward the side that is opposite the seam. The tension from this will help to keep the seam closed.

17. Stand each tamal, open end up, in a steamer basket, forming a circle of standing tamales leaning inward.

Corn and Beans

You may use a bowl in the center of the steamer to prop up the tamales. The water level in the steamer should not touch the tamales. When all the tamales are assembled and in the steamer, drop a penny on the bottom. The loud rattle of the penny will alert you that the water level is getting too low. Place any remaining wet corn husks on top, and then a kitchen towel and cover with a tight-fitting lid. Steam on high heat, for 45–50 minutes.

¡Buen provecho!

Tamales de Puerco | Pork Tamales
(makes a dozen tamales, or a few more if you stretch the *masa*)

Pork tamales are what we made for the Christmas and New Year's season. We made lots of them and when all the family gatherings were over in January, we still had tamales. To give the leftover tamales new life, *amá* would roast them on a *comal*, charring the husk black until the tamal was heated through. Try this the next time you want to reheat a tamal. The *masa* will roast slightly, become crispy, and you will discover a new taste of corn seasoned and roasted.

Ingredients
For Masa and Husks
3-1/2 ounces dried corn husks (*hojas de maíz*), about 26 separate husks, soaked in hot water for at least 30 minutes.
1 pound masa for tamales (Called *masa quebrada*, this is a coarser grind than *masa* for tortillas but not as coarse as cornmeal.)

1/2 cup canola oil or nonhydrogenated vegetable shortening
1/4–1/2 cup pork broth if needed

For the Chile Paste
3 ancho chiles, cleaned, seeded, and deveined
3 guajillo chiles, cleaned, seeded, and deveined
1 garlic clove
1/2 teaspoon ground cumin
3/4 cup water
1 tablespoon canola oil
1 teaspoon salt or to taste
1/2–1 cup of water as needed to blend the ingredients in a blender

For the Pork Filling
1 pound country-style pork ribs or pork shoulder
2 garlic cloves
1/2 white onion
1/4 teaspoon black peppercorns, crushed

Method
Place the corn husks in a large container and cover them with hot water. Let them soak and soften for at least 30 minutes and overnight if you like.

For the Pork
1. In a large pot, add the pork and cover it with water. Add the garlic, onion, and black peppercorns, and bring to a boil. Simmer on medium heat, uncovered, for 1-1/2 hours, skimming and discarding the foam that forms on the top.
2. When the pork is cooked, remove it from the broth, place it on a cutting board or large bowl, and cut

54

the meat into very small pieces so it looks like it has been shredded. Use a knife if necessary, just keep in mind that the texture of the pork should not be mushy.

3. Place the pork in a bowl and add 1/4 cup of the chile paste (below) and mix thoroughly. Set aside.

For the Chile Paste

4. To devein the chiles, first lay the chile flat on a cutting board and, using a paring knife, cut a slit lengthwise. Grab the chile with one hand and with the other remove the stem along with the bunch of seeds still attached to it. Open the chile along the slit and take out the remaining seeds and veins.

5. In a large saucepan, cover the cleaned chiles with water and bring to a boil. Turn off the heat and let the chiles steep for 15 minutes so that they rehydrate and become tender.

6. Drain the chiles and discard the water. Let the chiles cool a bit so as not to damage your blender, and then place the chiles in a blender along with the garlic, cumin, and salt. Blend to a very fine paste, adding about 1/2–1 cup water as needed.

7. In a Dutch oven, heat 1 tablespoon canola oil and fry the chile paste until it begins to change color and most of the liquid has evaporated. There will be splatter, so be prepared for it. Add 3/4 cup of water and simmer for about 15 minutes. The sauce will thicken and coat the back of a spoon.

For the Tamale Masa

8. In a stand mixer, using the paddle attachment, add 1/4 cup of the chile paste to the *masa* and mix thoroughly.

9. In a saucepan heat the canola oil or vegetable shortening to the point of shimmering. Adjust the mixer to low and slowly pour the hot oil into the masa to incorporate. It will sizzle as it makes contact. Watch out for splatter. When the oil is incorporated, turn up the mixer to medium and mix well. The batter should be slightly thicker than pancake or cake batter. Depending on how dry your *masa* is, you may need to add a little pork broth. You are ready to assemble the tamales.

Tradition dictates that by now family members and friends should be encircling you to help, be nosy, be a nuisance, and otherwise be themselves.

To Assemble the Tamales

10. Beginning 3 inches in from the pointed end of the husk, use a small spatula or spoon to spread about 3 tablespoons of *masa* on each corn husk. The masa will cover the husk thinly.

11. Spoon about 1-1/2 tablespoons of the shredded pork on the masa in a lengthwise strip, and then curl the husk lengthwise, tightly enveloping the filling.

12. Tightly fold the pointed tip toward the side that is opposite the seam. The tension from this will help to keep the seam closed.

13. Stand each tamal, open end up, in a steamer basket, forming a circle of standing tamales leaning inward. The water level in the steamer should not touch the tamales. You may use a bowl in the center of the steamer to prop up the tamales. When all the tamales are assembled and in the steamer, drop a penny on the bottom. The loud rattle of the penny will alert you that the water level is getting

too low. Place any remaining wet corn husks on top, followed by a kitchen towel, and cover with a tight-fitting lid. Steam on high heat, for 45–50 minutes. My sister Esther's husband, Juan Martinez, reminded me that the tamale masa will turn too dark if you overcook them.

¡Buen provecho!

Tamales de Res | Beef Tamales

(makes 12, or a few more if you stretch the *masa*)

Ingredients

For Masa and Husks

3-1/2 ounces dried corn husks (*hojas de maíz*), or about 26 separate husks, soaked in hot water for at least 30 minutes

1 pound *masa* for tamales, called *masa quebrada* (This is a coarser grind than *masa* for tortillas, but you do not want cornmeal.)

1/2 cup canola oil (I sometimes use organic palm oil shortening. It works really great and has no trans fats, since it is not hydrogenated. Also, as a solid fat it harkens back to pre-1500, before pigs, when fat came from nuts, fish, beavers, and other mammals with absolutely no lard.)

1/4–1/2 cup broth from the beef after it has been boiled

For the Beef Filling

1 pound boneless beef chuck

2 garlic cloves

1/2 teaspoon black peppercorns, crushed

2 sprigs (2 inches) of fresh Texas Mexican oregano (1/4 teaspoon dry)

For the Chile Paste

1 garlic clove

3 ancho chiles, cleaned, seeded, and deveined

3 guajillo chiles, cleaned, seeded, and deveined

1/2 teaspoon ground cumin

3/4 cups water

1 tablespoon canola oil

1 teaspoon salt or to taste

1/2–1 cup of water to blend the ingredients

Method

Place the corn husks in a large container and cover them with hot water. Let them soak and soften for at least 30 minutes or overnight if you like.

For the Beef

1. Place the beef in a Dutch oven and cover it with water. Add the garlic, black peppercorns, and oregano, and bring to a boil. Turn down the heat to very low so that it is barely simmering and cook for 2 hours.

2. When the beef is cooked, remove it from the broth, place it on a cutting board or large bowl, and, using forks or wooden spoons, pull the meat apart into very small pieces so that it looks like it has been shredded. Place the shredded beef in a skillet, add one cup of beef broth, cover, and hold warm until you add the chile paste.

3. When you have made the chile paste (see below), add 1/4 cup of the paste to the skillet of beef and mix well. Cook on medium, uncovered, for 15 minutes until most of the liquid has evaporated. Set aside.

Tamales de res.

For the Chile Paste

4. To devein the chiles, first lay the chile flat on a cutting board and, using a paring knife, cut a slit lengthwise. Then grab the chile with one hand and with the other break off the stem. Open the chile along the slit and take out the seeds and veins.

5. In a large saucepan, cover the cleaned chiles with water and bring to a boil. Turn off the heat and let the chiles steep for 15 minutes so that they rehydrate and become tender. Drain the chiles, discarding the water. Let the chiles cool a bit so as not to damage your blender.

6. Place the chiles in a blender along with the garlic, cumin, and salt. Blend to a very fine paste, adding water as needed. You will need to add 1/2–1 cup water.

7. In a Dutch oven, heat the tablespoon of canola oil and fry the chile paste until it begins to change color and most of the liquid has evaporated. There will be splatter, so be prepared for it. Add the 3/4 cup water and simmer for 15 minutes and adjust the salt. The paste should coat the back of a spoon, and have a complex, nongreen, nonpungent flavor. I think it tastes delicious.

For the Masa

8. In a stand mixer while using the paddle attachment, add 1/4 cup of the chile paste to the *masa* and mix thoroughly.

9. In a saucepan heat the shortening (or oil) to the point of shimmering. Adjust the mixer to low and slowly pour the hot oil into the *masa* to incorporate. It will sizzle as it makes contact. Watch out for splatter.

When the oil is incorporated, turn up the mixer to medium and mix well. The batter should be slightly thicker than pancake or cake batter. Depending on how dry your *masa* is, you may need to add a little of the beef broth to get the right texture for spreading. You are ready to assemble the tamales.

Tradition dictates that by now family members and friends should be encircling you to help. If they are not around, then you can be sure that they are making tamales in someone else's home and gossiping about you.

To Assemble the Tamales

10. Beginning 3 inches in from the pointed end of the husk, use a small spatula or spoon to spread about 2–3 tablespoons of *masa* on each corn husk. The masa will cover the husk thinly.

11. Spoon about 1-1/2 tablespoons of the shredded beef on the masa in a lengthwise strip, and then curl the husk lengthwise, enveloping the filling.

12. Fold the pointed tip up and stretch it toward the side opposite the seam. This tension will keep the seam closed. Stand each tamal, open end up, in a steamer basket, forming a circle of standing tamales leaning inward. You may use a small bowl in the center of the steamer to prop the tamales.

13. When all the tamales are assembled and in the steamer, drop a penny in the bottom of the steamer. The loud rattle of the penny will alert you that the water level is getting too low. Place some wet corn husks on the top, followed by a damp kitchen towel, and cover with a tight-fitting lid.

14. Steam on high heat, for 45–50 minutes.

Making these tamales will bring your family and extended family together for collaboration and enjoyment.

¡Buen provecho!

Tortillas de Harina | Wheat Tortillas
Recipe (makes 1-1/2 dozen)

Our wheat tortillas are fluffy and pliant. We always use a dash of baking powder. After listening over many years to heated debates about whether or not to put baking powder in wheat flour tortillas, I have come to believe that the debate is fundamentally about whether one believes that Texas Mexican exists as its own cuisine or whether it is an attempt to emulate south-of-the-border food. You can decide for yourself, given the long history of food in our region.

There are two main differences between our wheat flour tortillas and those of our sister regions in Northern Mexico. We use far less fat than they do and they do not use baking powder most of the time, although sometimes they do.

In this recipe I use a food processor because it is so much faster. I also give precise timing because it works for me. But there are so many variables to working with wheat flour that you will have to be attentive and find your way through the process. I think you will find the learning process worthwhile because these tortillas are really wonderfully soft and delicious. Almost like my mother's!

Ingredients
4 cups all-purpose wheat flour
1-1/2 teaspoons salt
1/2 teaspoon baking powder
1/2 cup palm oil shortening or other nonhydrogenated shortening
1 cup warm or hot water

Method
1. In a food processor, with the blade attachment, place the dry ingredients and pulse a couple of times.
2. Add the shortening and process until the shortening is completely blended, or about 10 seconds. There will be no granules, but if you squeeze the flour between your fingers, it will stick together.
3. Process again and as you do so, add the water slowly until the flour forms a ball of dough. This will take about 20 seconds.
4. Place the dough in a bowl and knead it with gusto for 6 minutes until it is shiny and definitely elastic. Set it aside to rest, covered, for 20 minutes.
5. Divide the dough into 18 balls. Form each ball into a little round pillow with an indentation in the middle. We still use the Nahuatl-based word for this, *testal*, which refers to the little ball of dough used to make corn tortillas (Lira Saade, 2005). The indentation in the middle and the fat edges will make rolling a snap.
6. On a floured surface, use a *palote* to roll each round tortilla to a thickness of 1/8 inch.
7. Heat a *comal* or griddle, ungreased, on high heat, 375°F–390°F. Place a tortilla on the *comal* and cook

59

Corn and Beans

for 30 seconds. Turn it over and cook another 30 seconds. Turn yet again and cook each side another 20–30 seconds.

Make sure that the tortilla is completely cooked. We do not eat raw or undercooked dough.

Tortillas de Maíz | Corn Tortillas

Recipe (makes 30 tortillas)

The tortilla.

Think of it as, well, not a wrap. Not a pita. Not bread, and certainly not a shell. Erase such conceptions and associations, and then take a fresh look at this iconic food. In culinary terms, an iconic food is one that is typical of a region and serves as a vehicle for understanding its people and culture.

Corn was first grown in Mexico starting in 5000–7000 BCE according to archaeological evidence found in caves around the Sierra de Tamaulipas between Monterrey and Mexico City and also in Tehuacán near today's Puebla (Gershenson, 2007). *Teosinte* is the native name of the early plant from which corn descended. Moving northward, corn was shared from one community to another and appeared in today's United States around 3500 BCE, according to archaeological evidence from a cave in New Mexico (Berzok, 2005).

It was shared among Native Americans with two cultural components that described how to grow it and how to eat it. Grow it alongside beans to replenish nitrogen in the soil. Eat it after it has been soaked in an alkali solution (ash from burning wood) that transforms the protein into a digestible form and boosts other nutrients. This process is called "nixtamalization," and the method is explained in the recipe for *pozole* (page 114).

When corn was transported to Europe in the 1500s, it traveled as a product dislocated from its history and culture. That was too bad because when you see only the product, you do not know how to grow it or how to eat it. Unfortunately this is still the case in the United States today.

Right now there is an important struggle revolving around corn. Some indigenous farmers in Mexico and the United States want the chemical and food giant, Monsanto, to stop planting genetically modified corn because they say it ruins the corn, the land, and their agricultural practices. Also, Greenpeace Mexico says that the mass production of corn flour, including the deployment of genetically modified organisms, is diminishing corn's nutrients. Greenpeace emphasizes the importance of nixtamalization and fears that dislocating corn from its culture will lead to widespread malnutrition (Ribeiro, 2012).

There is a growing number of U.S. chefs and home cooks who understand the nature of the tortilla, aware that it is a cultural heritage. We insist on cooking it in the traditional way that foregrounds its natural flavor, texture, and aroma. If you have never had a real corn tortilla, try this recipe and, my goodness, your mouth enjoyment will be a revelation.

A word about forming the tortillas. Although I keep practicing and prefer to make them by hand, I have yet to perfect the hand-shaping technique, slapping them back and forth between outstretched, water-moistened hands, as my mother did. If you are a serious cook, I suggest that you try to make tortillas by hand. We need

a new generation of trained cooks who make *tortillas hechas a mano* (hand-made tortillas). In the meantime, this recipe uses a tortilla press.

Ingredients

4 cups nixtamalized corn flour (You'll probably have to buy the Mexican brand, Maseca, which is the most readily available product in U.S. stores. Greenpeace Mexico asserts that it is made with genetically modified corn. Well, most U.S. grocery store food contains or is a genetically modified organism [Center for Food Safety, n.d.].)

3 cups water

1/2 teaspoon salt

Method

1. Add the salt to the flour and mix it in, and then add the water slowly as you mix with your hand to form a soft dough. It should be moist, soft, and give easily when you press it. Add a little more water or flour as necessary. Cover the dough with a damp cloth and let it stand for 30 minutes to make sure the corn is thoroughly rehydrated. At this stage you will notice the nice aroma of the corn.
2. Heat a *comal* (griddle) on medium high, 375°F.
3. Make 30 balls and flatten them, one by one, using a tortilla press lined with plastic. As you work, make sure to keep the *masa* balls covered with a damp cloth. The best plastic to use is a grocery store bag. Fold the plastic so that you have two layers and cut a piece that covers the surface of the press.
4. To flatten the tortilla, cover the bottom of the tortilla press with one half of the plastic and place one of the balls in the middle. Fold the other half of the plastic over the ball. Press once, gently. Then turn the plastic-wrapped tortilla 180° and press a second time, firmly.
5. Steps from press to comal:
   A. Gently peel off the plastic from the top of the tortilla.
   B. Use the bottom plastic to remove the tortilla from the press and place the uncovered side in your right hand, assuming that you are right handed.
   C. With your left hand carefully and gently peel off the plastic from the other side.
   D. Release the tortilla from your palm as you roll it onto the comal.
6. Cook it for about 30 seconds. Then use a spatula to flip it and cook the other side for 30 seconds. The tortilla will bubble up. The outer leaf will be slightly crispy and the inside will be smooth and buttery. If you overcook the tortilla, it will be dry and yucky. Keep the cooked tortillas in a bowl, covered with cloth to retain the moisture.

Try serving as a *machito*. I believe my *amá* made up that name, but I'm not sure. She would take the tortilla right off the griddle and with her fingers sprinkle droplets of water on it, as if sprinkling magic. Roll it and squeeze it into a moist, steaming little cigar. Fresh corn aroma, roasted flavor, moist, creamy texture. I ate it with gusto. I must have been five years old.

Serve these tortillas with scrambled eggs. Or make a taco using only salted avocado slices. Or only beans. Or eat them with just a bit of serrano salsa. There's nothing quite like the creamy texture, the crisped overleaf, and the unique roasted taste and aroma of a fresh corn tortilla.

5
CHILES, SALSAS, AND GUACAMOLES

**Chile Anaheim con Tortillas de Maíz y Queso |
Anaheim Chiles with Corn Tortillas and Cheese**
Recipe (serves 8)

Direct, uncomplicated, profuse flavor.

I think oftentimes we miss so much by complicating our every day, wasting time with artifice. I recommend to every cook: just look at the beauty of what's around you, get real, and go with it!

We roast Anaheim chiles and then eat them with hot yellow corn tortillas and salt. Nothing else. There's not a single gourmand who can resist crooning with joy upon biting into this. Roast the chiles, add salt, and eat them with a yellow corn tortilla! Here is the step-by-step method.

Ingredients
10 fresh Anaheim chiles
Corn tortillas
Salt to taste
Panela cheese, cut into 1/4-inch cubes
Asadero cheese, cut into 3-inch by 1/4-inch strips

Method

For the Chile

1. On a *comal* or cast-iron griddle, roast the chiles until most of the surface is charred. You can use a broiler or an open fire. But for this recipe I find that the extended time it takes to char on the comal is just right for cooking the inside of the chile. There's still texture but it's not at all firm. You don't want to bite into a raw, firm chile. Let's not get lost in the crudité 1980s again.
2. Place them in a paper bag and close tightly so that the moisture helps release the skin.
3. When cool enough to handle, peel off the skin and remove the seeds. Slice the chiles lengthwise into 1-inch–wide strips (*rajas*).

For the Tortilla

If you make fresh tortillas, you have a place in heaven, but if you buy them from the store, dip them in water as explained below to make them taste nearly freshly made.

4. For store-bought tortillas: in a wide-mouthed shallow bowl filled with water, immerse the corn tortillas for 30 seconds or longer, up to several minutes.
5. Heat a clean *comal* or griddle on high, to the point that when you sprinkle droplets of water they dance on the surface.
6. Place the hydrated tortillas on the griddle and cook one side for about 10–15 seconds. The tortillas should char just a little bit but you don't want them to burn. Turn over with a spatula and now you will add the chiles.

Roasted Anaheim chile.

Roasted Anaheim chile and yellow corn tortilla.

Roasted Anaheim chiles with *queso asadero* in yellow corn tortillas.

7. Place *rajas* of the chiles on half of the tortilla, sprinkle with salt, and fold in half. Heat for about 10 seconds, and then turn it over and heat the other half of the tortilla. This roasts the tortilla and also reheats the chile nicely.

Serve immediately, while they are aromatic and steamy. Yes, you can add cheese if you like, but only after you have tasted them straight.

I recommend two cheeses—good melting asadero and more delicately flavored panela that melts less readily. I believe that both are available in most supermarkets in the United States. I wouldn't use longhorn or cheddar. Too loud.

Add the cheese after sprinkling the salt on the *rajas* as indicated above, and then fold the tortilla and proceed, also as above. Both cheeses will melt well, but differently. Remember that we want to taste primarily the chile's shades of flavor.

Chile Ancho Adobo

Recipe (makes 3 cups)

Adobos are delicious sauces and marinades, blends of chiles, an acid, sugar, and specially selected spices. I add *piloncillo* and some nontraditional spices to this Texas Mexican version, and I find it matches beautifully with smoked and grilled meats, such as pork loin (see page 116).

Ingredients

For the Chile Purée

4 large ancho chiles, deveined and deseeded
1 pasilla chile, deveined and deseeded
2 cloves garlic
4 cups water for boiling the chiles
1 cup water
1 tablespoon canola oil

For the Adobo

2 tomatoes
1 tablespoon canola oil
1 small onion, diced
1/2 rib celery, diced
1/2 cup firmly packed piloncillo
3/4 cup apple cider vinegar
6 tablespoons chile purée (from above)
1 teaspoon salt

Method

For the Chile Purée, Base of Adobo

1. To devein the chiles, first lay the chile flat on a cutting board and, using a paring knife, cut a slit lengthwise. Grab the chile with one hand and with the other remove the stem along with the bunch of seeds still attached to it. Open the chile along the slit and take out the remaining seeds and veins.

2. In a large saucepan, cover the cleaned chiles with water and bring to a boil. Turn off the heat and let the chiles steep for 15 minutes so that they rehydrate and become tender.

3. Drain the chiles, discarding the water. Let the chiles cool a bit so as not to damage your blender. Place the chiles in a blender along with the garlic. Blend to a very fine paste, adding about 1/2–1 cup water as needed.

4. In a Dutch oven, heat 1 tablespoon canola oil and fry the chile paste until the color deepens and most of the liquid has evaporated. There will be splatter, so be prepared for it. Add 1 cup of water and simmer for 15–20 minutes. The sauce will thicken to the point that it coats the back of a spoon.

For the Adobo

5. In a sauté pan heat 1 tablespoon canola oil and sauté the diced onions and the celery until they are soft.

6. In a blender, place the sautéed onions, celery, 6 tablespoons of the chile purée and all of the remaining ingredients. Blend on high until completely smooth.

Serve immediately or keep refrigerated for up to 6 days. The taste is sweet, pungent, and aromatic with the ancho chiles. Serve as an *adobo* for roast chicken at dinner or for smoked meats at an afternoon barbecue.

Chile con Queso | Chile with Cheese
Recipe (makes 1-1/2 cups)

Ingredients
   3 poblano chiles, charred, peeled, and deseeded
   1 tablespoon canola oil or other vegetable oil
   1/2 white onion, thinly sliced
   1 Roma tomato, diced small
   3 tablespoons *crema mexicana* (If you cannot find crema mexicana, you can substitute *crème fraîche*.)

Chile con queso.

3 tablespoons whole milk

4 ounces Chihuahua cheese, cut into small cubes

1/4 teaspoon salt

Method

1. Place the chiles under a broiler, turning them so that they are entirely charred and the skin is blistered. Place them in a paper bag, close tightly, and let them sweat for 15 minutes so that the skin will be easier to peel off.

2. Place each chile on a cutting board and peel off the skin with your fingers. You can use a dull knife if you need to gently scrape off some of the skin, but this should not be necessary if the chiles are well charred.

3. On the cutting board, cut a slit lengthwise in each chile. Open the chile and lay it flat, inside flesh facing up. Remove the stem and the cluster of seeds attached to it. Remove the remaining seeds by sliding them away gently with your finger or a butter knife.

4. Cut the chiles into strips, *rajas*, 1/4–1/2 inch wide and 2 inches long. Set aside.

5. Heat the oil in a skillet, medium heat, and add the thinly sliced onions. Cook them slowly until they are transparent but still completely white with no brown or golden color. Add the diced tomatoes, poblano strips, salt, and cook for 3 minutes. Then turn the heat to low.

6. In a cup or small bowl, whisk together the milk and the crema mexicana, pour into the chile mixture, and blend. Turn off the heat. Add the cheese, blend it, and allow it to melt. Adjust the salt.

Serve immediately with hot corn or wheat tortillas.

Chile Relleno | Stuffed Poblano Chiles (Two Versions)

Recipe (serves 6)

This is a dish for dinner parties. For the *lampreado* (battered) version, the chiles can be stuffed and held in a warm oven until the moment when they are battered and fried. The natural version will not require any last-minute preparation.

For the nonbattered version, you can stuff the chiles, arrange them in a casserole dish, and refrigerate them several hours before your party. Then, about 30–45 minutes before you are ready to serve, just add the *caldito*, cover, and pop in the oven until bubbly.

Ingredients

6 fresh, firm poblano chiles

1 pound ground sirloin

1 tablespoon canola oil

1/8 teaspoon black peppercorns

1/8 teaspoon salt

1 teaspoon garlic, minced

2 tablespoons raisins

2 tablespoons pecans, roasted in a 350°F oven for 8 minutes

1 cup water

For the Tomato Caldito (Soup, Juice)

8 Roma tomatoes

1/4 small white onion, peeled

1/2 teaspoon fresh Mexican oregano

1 garlic clove

1/8 teaspoon salt

2 tablespoons peanut or canola oil

Chile relleno.

For the Batter

10 ounces all-purpose flour (2-1/2 cups)
1/2 teaspoon baking powder
1 teaspoon salt
1 egg
16 fluid ounces water
1/2 cup additional flour for dredging

Method

For the Chiles

1. Place the chiles under a broiler, turning them so that they are entirely charred and the skin has blistered. Place them in a paper bag, close tightly, and let them sweat for 15 minutes so that they will be easier to peel.
2. Place each chile flat on a cutting board and peel off the skin with your fingers. You can use a dull knife if you need to gently scrape off some of the skin, but this should not be necessary if the chiles are well charred.
3. Keeping the chile flat, cut a slit lengthwise in each chile, and gently remove all the seeds. Do not remove the stem. You will find a big cluster of seeds just inside attached to the stem. You can use a small knife to cut off this cluster of seeds if you cannot break it off with your fingers. Set the cleaned chiles aside.

For the Beef Filling

4. Place the salt, garlic, and black peppercorns in a *molcajete* and grind into a smooth paste. Add 1/4 cup water and set aside.
5. Heat the canola oil in a skillet at medium heat. Add the beef and cook for 8–10 minutes until it has browned. Add the *molcajete* paste, the rest of the water, and deglaze by scraping off the browned bits at the bottom of the skillet with a wooden spatula or spoon. Cook for another 8 minutes. Add the roasted pecans and raisins and continue to cook until the raisins are plump and most of the liquid is gone. Set side.

For the Caldito

6. In a saucepan cover the tomatoes with water and boil them for 10–15 minutes until they are completely cooked, with the skin peeling off. Drain and reserve the liquid.
7. Place the cooked tomatoes, garlic, and onion in a blender and purée.
8. Heat the oil in a Dutch oven and add the tomato purée slowly and carefully because the tomato will splatter when it meets the hot oil. Cook on medium, stirring, for 5 minutes. Add 1 cup of the water from the cooked tomatoes and the oregano, and simmer for 15 minutes. The consistency should be that of a thin soup. Keep the caldito hot until you are ready to assemble.

Assemble the Chiles for *Natural* Version

9. After you have cleaned all the chiles, fill them with the ground beef filling, place them seam side down in a casserole, and cover them with the *caldito*.
10. Bake in 350°F oven for 25–30 minutes or until they are thoroughly heated. Serve with hot corn tortillas. You can assemble them, without adding the caldito, and hold in the refrigerator for 3–4 hours. Before serving, just pour the caldito over the chiles, cover, and

heat in the oven until the caldito starts to bubble, and the chiles are thoroughly heated, from 30–45 minutes.

Assemble the Chiles for *Lampreado (Battered)* **Version**

9. In a bowl, whisk together the dry ingredients.
10. Beat the egg and water together, add to the dry ingredients, and whisk until the batter is smooth.
11. Place about 1/2 cup of flour in a large plate and lightly coat the exterior of each stuffed chile, shaking off excess. They are now ready for dipping and frying.
12. In a deep skillet add vegetable oil to a 1-1/2–inch depth and heat to the point that it is shimmering (350°F).
13. Using a spatula and tongs, dip each flour-coated, stuffed chile into the batter, place in the skillet, and fry each side for 2 minutes until golden brown. Place on paper towels to drain

To serve, place each chile on a plate and pour plenty of the hot caldito over each one. To say that this is heaven is no exaggeration.

Guacamole

Recipe (serves 6)

Avocado in Spanish is *aguacate*, derived from the original Nahuatl name, *ahucacahuitl*. The name appears in early writings and in Mesoamerican hieroglyphs, including glyphs from the Codex Mendoza of an avocado tree linked to the place where the tree originates, the town of Ahuacatlán. The earliest remains of avocado consumption dated to 8000–7000 BCE, were found in a cave in present-day Coxcatlán, in Puebla, Mexico.

Three types of avocados named for the regions in which they flourished. Courtesy of Hofshi Foundation, avocadosource.com.

There are three botanical types of aguacate: Mexican, Guatemalan, and Antillean (Sánchez-Colín, Mijares-Oviedo, López-López, and Barrientos-Priego, 2001). The region where the Mexican type developed includes the terrain that Texas indigenous people frequented, either because they were fleeing Texas or raiding for food and goods.

I have three rules for making good guacamole:

1. Purchase avocados when they are green and hard. This is the advice from Rodolfo Fernandez, my sister Gloria's husband, who in my opinion is the top avocado expert in our region. For many years his produce company provided the best-tasting avocados to Mexican restaurants throughout San Antonio. Purchase Haas aguacates while they are still green and very firm. Store them in a plastic or paper bag and wait 2 days, maybe 3, at which time they will have ripened and become slightly soft to the touch. It is then that they are at their flavor peak.
2. No masks. The fresh, full flavor of the avocado takes nicely to complementary seasonings and accompa-

niments, but be judicious. At all costs do not mask the texture or flavor of the *aguacate*.

3. Use a *molcajete* to make a paste of the flavors that you want in your guacamole, and then add the cut-up avocado and blend. This ensures that the flavors are evenly distributed.

Ingredients

2 Haas avocados, diced
1/2 tablespoon green serrano chile, sliced
1/2 tablespoon fresh cilantro, finely chopped
1 teaspoon white onion, small dice
1 teaspoon salt
1/4 cup tomato, small dice
2 tablespoons white onion, small dice
2 tablespoons fresh cilantro, coarsely chopped

Method

1. Using a *molcajete*, make a fine paste of 1 teaspoon onion, the chile, 1/2 tablespoon cilantro, and salt. Here is where I mentioned that you can develop the flavor direction that your guacamole will take. You may add other seasonings to the molcajete, but keep in mind that you are following many years of tradition. Make sure that your variations are culturally relevant, enticing to the palette, and not just vacuously trendy.

2. Dice the avocado and add to the molcajete, scraping and folding to ensure that the avocado is covered with the paste.

3. Add the remaining tomato, cilantro, and onion. Adjust the salt.

Serve immediately with corn tortillas or with crispy corn tortilla chips.

Guacamole con Frutas | Guacamole with Fruit
Recipe (serves 6)

This is a beautiful blending of avocado with crisp tart grapes and pomegranates. A Guanajuato and Morelos recipe (Santibañez, 2007), I include it here because I love the twist it gives to the general way that we serve guacamole. As Texas Mexican cuisine evolves, there surely will be continued sharing of recipes among the regions, as there was in the past.

Ingredients

2 Haas avocados, diced
3/4 cup fresh mango, small cubes
10 red seedless grapes, halved
10 green seedless grapes, halved
1/2 cup pomegranate seeds
1/2 tablespoon green serrano chile, sliced (Note: I like to add more chile than this because I love the sweet fruit taste with the serrano flavor. But start with this amount and then see if you want to increase the serrano flavor.)
1/4 cup tomato, small dice
1 teaspoon white onion, diced
1 teaspoon salt

Method

1. Using a *molcajete*, make a fine paste of the onion, chile, and salt.

2. Dice the avocado and add to the molcajete, scraping and folding to ensure that the avocado is covered with the paste. The avocado diced pieces should hold their shape.

3. After combining the avocados with the molcajete paste, fold in the tomatoes and the fruit.
4. Adjust the salt. Garnish with additional pomegranate and serve with crispy corn tortilla chips.

Mole Poblano
Recipe (serves 16)

Mole practically solemnized every one of my family's weddings. It was traditional. I made it for my sister, Gloria Fernandez, on her wedding anniversary just before she passed away. I'll never forget the exquisite smile on her face as she savored my gift to her. That communicative smile was her gift to me.

We always served mole with chicken. Following is the recipe for my mole poblano, which is as close as I can get to my mother's mole.

I find that it is easier to learn to make a mole if you think of the types or groups of ingredients as you would an instrument section in a symphony orchestra. If each group is to bring its special character and tone to the mole, the ingredients must be well prepared—tuned as it were—prior to blending.

Ingredients
Aromatics
These aromatics are to be fried in a bare minimum of canola oil to the point when they begin to release their aroma.

14 black peppercorns
5 cloves, whole
1 3-inch stick of Mexican *canela* (cinnamon)
1/2 teaspoon coriander seeds
1/2 teaspoon anise seeds

Nuts, Seeds, and Grain
These are to be fried in a small amount of canola oil, each separately, to the point of golden. The pumpkin seeds turn bitter if overcooked, so be attentive.

20 almonds
2 ounces pumpkin seeds
1/2 cup brown sesame seeds
Chile seeds from the cleaned chiles below
1 corn tortilla, stale

Vegetables and Fruit
The tomatoes are to be fried in a small amount of canola oil in high heat to caramelize the starches, and the raisins are plumped, also in the oil.

The onion and garlic are roasted in a dry cast-iron skillet or *comal*. Black spots and softness will tell you that they are ready. Peel off the skin from the garlic after it is cooked.

1 white onion, cut in half
3 garlic cloves, unpeeled
4 Roma tomatoes, quartered
6 tomatillos, quartered
3 teaspoons black raisins

The Chiles
Wipe them clean, and seed and devein them. Reserve the chile seeds for frying as mentioned above.

The following are the main attraction in this sumptuous mole:

8 mulato chiles, seeded and deveined
5 ancho chiles, seeded and deveined
6 pasilla chiles, seeded and deveined
2 chipotle chiles, seeded and deveined

Onion and garlic roasted on a dry, cast-iron skillet for *mole poblano*.

Chocolate

Use 5 ounces Mexican chocolate. Don't use plain cacao. The Mexican chocolate has the necessary sugar and additional canela flavor.

Additional salt, to taste, and sugar will be added at the end.

Chicken and Remaining Ingredients

1 chicken, skin removed, cut up into small pieces according to your preference.

1/2–3/4 cup canola or other vegetable oil (The oil will be used, several tablespoons at a time, to fry the various ingredients during preparation of the mole.)

2 teaspoons salt, or to taste

Method

1. To devein the chiles, first lay the chile flat on a cutting board and, using a paring knife, cut a slit lengthwise. Grab the chile with one hand and with the other remove the stem along with the bunch of seeds still attached to it. Open the chile along the slit and take out the remaining seeds and veins. Save all the seeds in a bowl and discard the veins.

2. Fry the deveined, deseeded chiles on both sides in 2 tablespoons canola oil until they begin to blister.

3. In a large saucepan, cover the fried chiles with water and bring to a boil. Turn off the heat and let the chiles steep for 15 minutes so that they rehydrate and become tender. Drain them, discarding the water. After they cool a bit, place them in a blender, add a cup of water, and blend on high until blended into a thoroughly smooth purée. Add more water as needed to blend properly. You may need to do this in batches. Set aside.

4. Fry the tomatoes and tomatillos in the oil remaining from the chiles, adding a bit more if necessary. Set aside.

5. Using 4 tablespoons of the oil, fry the raisins until they are plump. Remove the raisins, and then fry each of the following ingredients separately (not together in a single batch): almonds, pumpkin seeds, tortillas, reserved chile seeds, and sesame seeds. Set aside.

6. Roast the onion and garlic on a dry *comal* or skillet (i.e., no oil) over medium heat. Remove the garlic from the griddle when the skin begins to brown. Peel it and discard the skin. Keep turning the onion until it is soft and has black spots on all sides. Remove from heat and set aside.

7. In a small skillet, add enough oil to fry, over medium low heat, the black pepper, cloves, cinnamon, coriander, and anise seeds, all together, until fragrant. Remove from heat and set aside.

8. In a blender, blend the dry-roasted vegetables, spices, and fried ingredients in batches, adding fresh water as needed, to form a smooth purée. Be patient and let the blender smooth away. If after blending you find that there are grainy particles, strain through a fine-mesh sieve. Set aside.

9. Cover one cut-up chicken with water and bring it to a boil. Turn down the heat to medium low and cook at a bare simmer, no rapid boiling, for 40 minutes until the chicken is done. Set aside. Do not discard the chicken broth.

10. Heat 3 tablespoons of oil in a Dutch oven over

medium heat. Add the chile purée slowly and with caution because it will splatter. Stir frequently until the color deepens and you can see the bottom of the pan when scraped with a wooden spoon, about 8 minutes. Add the puréed vegetable and spice mixture. Reduce heat to a simmer and stir occasionally until the mole thickens, about 1 hour.

11. Add approximately 2 cups of the chicken broth to the mole and cook for another 30 minutes. The mole should coat the back of a spoon. Add the chocolate pieces and continue cooking, about 10 minutes. Add the salt and adjust to taste. Add 1/4–1/2 teaspoon sugar as needed.

12. Add the chicken pieces and cook on a bare simmer for 10–15 minutes until the chicken is heated through.

Serve the chicken pieces with plenty of the mole and sprinkle sesame seeds on top. We served it with Texas Mexican rice and corn tortillas.

The mole will keep in the refrigerator for 2 weeks. You can also freeze it and it will be fine for up to 2 months.

Papas con Rajas | Potatoes with Poblano Chile Strips

Recipe (serves 4)

Ingredients

4 small waxy potatoes, peeled and cut into 1/2-inch cubes (about 2-1/2 cups) (I like Yukon gold, but you can use any kind except russet.)

2 poblano chiles

Papas con rajas.

1/2 white onion, peeled and sliced thinly

2 tablespoons canola or other vegetable oil

Salt to taste

Method

1. Place the chiles under a broiler, turning them so that they are entirely charred and the skin blisters. Place them in a paper bag, close tightly, and let them sweat for 15 minutes so that the skin will be easier to peel off.

2. Place each chile on a cutting board and peel off the skin with your fingers. You can use a dull knife if you need to gently scrape off some of the skin, but this should not be necessary if the chiles are well charred.

3. On the cutting board, cut a slit lengthwise in each chile. Open the chile and lay it flat, inside flesh facing up. Remove the stem and the cluster of seeds attached to it. Remove the remaining seeds by sliding them away gently with your finger or a butter knife.

4. Cut the chiles into strips, 1/4–1/2 inch wide and 2 inches long. Set aside.

5. Peel the potatoes and cut into 1/2-inch cubes.

6. Fill a large pot with water and bring it to a boil, and then add the potato cubes and cook for 5 minutes. By that time they should be partially cooked. Take a cube out and test it, cutting into it to ensure that it is still somewhat firm in the center. If it is too hard, let it cook for another minute. Drain in a colander.

7. In a 12-inch skillet, preferably nonstick, heat the oil over medium heat. Add the onions and cook for about 3 minutes until they begin to turn translucent.

Add the potatoes and let them heat through and acquire some golden color, about another 3 minutes. Then add the *rajas* and cook for an additional 2 minutes until heated through.

Serve piping hot.

Rajas Poblanas | Poblano Strips
Recipe (serves 6 as appetizer)

This is a great appetizer for company. In this recipe, you mix the earthy flavor of poblano chiles with smooth *crema mexicana*. Once you make it you will see that it resembles the Texas Mexican *chile con queso*. Both combine chiles with cream and cheese for contrast in taste and mouth feel. I sometimes like to serve *rajas poblanas* and *chile con queso* (page 67) side by side to savor the interesting differences.

Ingredients

4 poblano chiles

1 white onion, sliced into 1/4-inch strips

1 tablespoon canola oil

3/4 cup *crema mexicana* (Use *crème fraîche* if you cannot find crema mexicana.)

1/2 cup panela cheese, cut into 1/2-inch cubes

Salt to taste

Method

1. Place the chiles under a broiler, turning them so that they are entirely charred and the skin blisters. Place them in a paper bag, close tightly and let them sweat for 15 minutes so that the skin will be easier to peel off.

2. Place each chile on a cutting board and peel off the skin with your fingers. You can use a dull knife if you need to gently scrape off some of the skin, but this should not be necessary if the chiles are well charred.

3. On the cutting board, cut a slit lengthwise in each chile. Open the chile and lay it flat, inside flesh facing up. Remove the stem and the cluster of seeds attached to it. Remove the remaining seeds by sliding them away gently with your finger or a butter knife.

4. Cut the chiles lengthwise into strips, 1/4–1/2 inch wide. Set aside.

5. Heat the oil in a skillet over medium heat, add the onion slices, and sauté until they soften, about 4 minutes.

6. Reduce the heat to low, add the chiles and the crema mexicana, and heat them thoroughly. Add the panela cubes and stir gently. Adjust the salt.

Serve the *rajas* with hot corn tortillas, of course. Warning: You may uncontrollably crave a margarita!

Salsa de Chile Serrano con Aguacate | Serrano Chile and Avocado Salsa

Recipe (makes 2 cups)

Our cuisine is more adaptive than the meal-sequencing categories that come from Europe, such as appetizer, salad, entrée, and dessert. In our home we enjoyed combinations of foods or lone dishes with no sequencing needed. During the day we would often eat small portions of this or that treat placed on the table or on the stove, with no time nor social categories such as the English teatime or the Spanish *merienda*. It was a rhythm of eating small portions throughout the day.

I was about 6 years old and clearly remember an early afternoon when I saw the *molcajete* and beautiful bright green chunks on our kitchen table. I thought it was avocado, which I loved, so I put some in a corn tortilla and took a bite. Pain! I had discovered chile. After my torment subsided, I thought to myself, "who would ruin avocado with a mouth-burning ingredient?" Well I soon learned to love this salsa, which could also double as a guacamole dip if your family likes piquant as I now do. This recipe is always a hit when I bring it to family gatherings.

Ingredients
2 serrano chiles, sliced into circles
2 Haas avocados
1/4 teaspoon salt

Method
1. Place the serrano chiles and salt in a *molcajete* and mash into a fine paste.
2. Cut the avocado in half, remove the seed, and, with a butter knife, score each half into small cubes. Spoon out the flesh cubes from the avocado halves onto the *molcajete* and blend together. Adjust the salt.

Nothing could be simpler because these two flavors just go together so naturally. Spread it on a freshly made corn tortilla and, *ay, dios mío*, that's how you spell *delicioso*!

Salsa de Chile de Arbol
Recipe (makes 1 cup)

When you want an aromatic salsa on the table, use this chile de arbol. The flavor is similar to that of the serrano, although unlike the serrano, *chile de arbol* is used mainly in its dried form. The name "chile of a tree" does not mean that the chile grows on a tree but merely implies that this chile plant is taller than other chile plants. Also called *chile arbol* all over Texas, it is one of the most commonly used chiles in table salsa and, as you'll find upon making the recipe below, has an enticing aroma and vibrant red color.

Ingredients
1 chile de arbol
1/8 teaspoon salt
1/2 tablespoons white onion, diced
2 Roma tomatoes, canned or fresh, roughly cut up

Method
1. Place the chile de arbol, salt, and onion in a *molcajete* and grind to a smooth paste.
2. Add the tomatoes and smash to your heart's content, blending all the ingredients. Yes, it's that simple. But the flavors are complex and earthy. Enjoy!

Fried Chile de Arbol Salsa
Recipe (makes 2 cups)

Variations for developing flavor in chiles for *adobo*s, moles, or salsas are numerous. In this salsa, the flavor

Fried *chile de arbol*, onions, and garlic for salsa.

of the *chile de arbol* is deepened by frying it together with onion and garlic. When it is served, the black flecks in the salsa make it look rustic, and I can even detect some smokiness in the flavor.

Ingredients

2 chile de arbol
1/4 teaspoon salt
2 tablespoons white onion, diced
1 tablespoon canola or vegetable oil
4 Roma tomatoes, canned or fresh, roughly cut up

Method

1. Heat the oil in a skillet, add the chile de arbol, onion, and garlic, and fry them until the chile darkens in color and the onions are soft, about 3–4 minutes. Remove from the skillet and set aside to cool.
2. Add the tomatoes to the same skillet and cook for 4 minutes on medium heat. Remove and set aside to cool.
3. When the ingredients are cool, place them in a blender and blend until you have a smooth purée. There will still be some small flecks of the fried chile, adding nice texture and color to the salsa.

This is the salsa that you'll want to add to any type of grilled fish or meats. Make a batch and keep it handy in the fridge. It will keep for 7 days.

Salsa Verde Cocida | Cooked Green Salsa

Recipe (makes 1-1/2 cups)

Ingredients

8 ounces tomatillos, about 3 medium tomatillos
1 *chile jalapeño* (Sometimes these chiles can be large, and that is just fine for those who like hot salsas.)
1 small garlic clove
1/4 white onion
1/4 cup fresh cilantro, coarsely chopped
1/4 teaspoon salt

Method

1. Place the tomatillos, chiles, garlic, and onion in a saucepan. Cover with water and boil for about 10 minutes or until the chile turns a pale green and the tomatoes are completely cooked, with the skin peeling off.
2. Drain and let the ingredients cool.
3. When cool, place in a blender, add the cilantro and salt, and blend on medium until the salsa is smooth but with some of the seeds still intact.

Salsa de Chile Serrano y Tomate | Serrano Chile and Tomato Salsa

Recipe (makes 1 cup)

Ingredients

3 tablespoons *serrano chile*, sliced into circles
2 fresh tomatoes, diced (Sometimes we did not have fresh tomatoes so *amá* would use 3/4 cup canned tomato sauce.)
1/8 teaspoon salt

Method

1. Place serrano chile and salt in a *molcajete* and mash into a fine paste.
2. Add the diced tomatoes and mash together. If using tomato sauce, pour it into the molcajete and blend with the chile paste.

Both fresh-tomato and tomato-sauce versions bring back pleasant memories of home, the plentiful times and the lean times.

Salsa Mexicana a.k.a. Pico de Gallo

Recipe (makes 1-1/2 cups)

This is called "*salsa mexicana*" in Mexico due to its colors matching those of the Mexican flag. There are two rules to follow that will keep this, your terrific and bright salsa, from looking and tasting like a lame, limp, leftover hodgepodge.

First, try your best to dice the tomato and onion evenly and small. The uniform pieces will not only look great but they will have a much better mouth feel and distribution of taste.

Second, use the freshest ingredients you can find. This salsa depends on brightness: the refreshing contrast of tomato with onion, perked by the earthy taste of serrano and finishing with the aroma of cilantro. The lime and salt raise the volume on each ingredient. If you do it right, this is a heady, brilliant salsa.

Ingredients

1 cup ripe tomato, small dice (Do not store tomatoes in the refrigerator. The cold destroys the enzymes in tomatoes that produce the fresh flavor and it also turns the flesh from crisp to mealy.)

3 tablespoons white onion, small dice

3 tablespoons finely minced serrano chile

1/4 cup fresh cilantro, coarsely chopped

1 teaspoon fresh lime juice

1/4 teaspoon salt

Method

Simplicity. Mix together all of the fresh ingredients and adjust the salt.

Salsa Ranchera

Recipe (makes 1-1/2 cups)

This salsa is truly a cornerstone of our cuisine. There is no substitute for its unique taste. I taste it and am instantly and completely transported to my childhood home and family. The combination of flavors is really that distinctive and powerful.

Ingredients

2 Roma tomatoes

1 chile serrano

1-1/2 ounces white onion (3 tablespoons by volume)

1 small garlic clove

1/4 teaspoon salt

Method

1. Place all the ingredients, except the salt, in a pan of boiling water and cook for about 10 minutes. The chile begins to turn a pale green and the tomatoes

are completely cooked but not falling apart. Drain
and let the ingredients cool.

2. When cool, place in a blender, add the salt and blend
on medium until the salsa is smooth. There will still
be some seeds present. I like that.

Compare this salsa with others in a taste test exercise,
and you will understand how original and unique it
is. Two ancient techniques are involved: boiling and
blending. And to think that the flavor comes from a
very simple combination of only four ingredients, two
of them indigenous and two of them imported.

Clockwise starting at the top: *salsa verde cocida*, *salsa de chile serrano y tomate*, *salsa ranchera*, and *pico de gallo*.

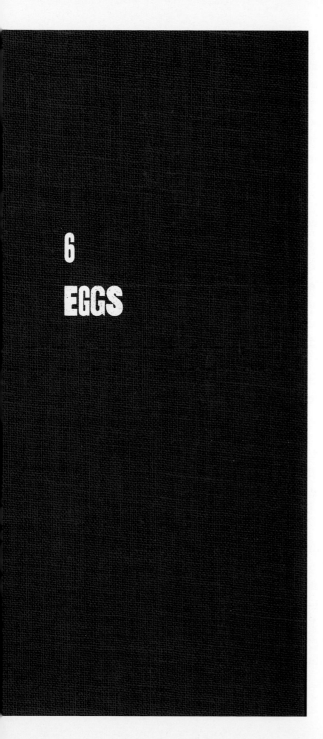

6

EGGS

Chorizo con Huevo | Mexican Chorizo and Eggs
Recipe for Chorizo (makes 3-1/4 pounds)

Chorizo is the creative culinary result of imported pigs meeting the local chiles. A gay, fortuitous marriage. It is famous, of course, as a breakfast treat but you can also serve it as a spicy, aromatic topping on *cazuelitas* (page 37). This recipe includes cinnamon and cloves but some families in south Texas do not use any aromatics at all. Also, some families use apple cider vinegar instead of the white vinegar in my recipe.

I think that once you try this recipe you'll want to regularly make chorizo rather than buy it. You can leave out all that extra fat found in store-bought chorizo, and it is not very complicated to make and store. I don't use casings because they are unnecessary. I store the seasoned chorizo in plastic zip-lock bags and pop them into the freezer, ready for later use.

Ingredients
8 ancho chiles, seeds and veins removed
5 pasilla chiles, seeds and veins removed
3 pounds lean ground pork
1 cup white vinegar
3 cloves garlic, peeled
1/2 tablespoon ground black pepper

1-1/2 tablespoons salt

1/2 teaspoon ground cumin

3 cloves

1/4 teaspoon ground cinnamon

Method

1. To devein the chiles, first lay the chile flat on a cutting board and, using a paring knife, cut a slit lengthwise. Grab the chile with one hand and with the other remove the stem along with the bunch of seeds still attached to it. Open the chile along the slit and take out the remaining seeds and veins.

2. In a large saucepan, cover the cleaned chiles with water and bring to a boil. Turn off the heat and let the chiles steep for 15 minutes so that they rehydrate and become tender. Drain the chiles, discarding the water. Let the chiles cool a bit so as not to damage your blender, and then place the chiles in a blender along with the vinegar, garlic, black pepper, salt, cumin, cloves, and cinnamon. Blend on high for several minutes until you have a smooth paste.

3. In a large bowl, add the chile paste to the lean ground pork and mix well. Refrigerate for 24 hours to let all the flavors blend.

4. Divide the chorizo into small batches that are just the right size for later servings. Stored in the freezer they will keep for up to 3 months.

To Make Chorizo and Eggs

Method

1. In a nonstick skillet, cook 1/4 cup of chorizo on medium heat until it is completely cooked.

2. Lower the heat to low and then add 2 eggs. I always discard one of the egg yolks.

3. Scramble the eggs to combine with the chorizo. Cook slowly just until the eggs are cooked without becoming dry.

Serve immediately with hot, wheat flour tortillas for tacos.

Papas con Huevo | Potato and Egg Taco

Recipe (serves 4)

Ingredients

4 small waxy potatoes, peeled and cut into 1/2-inch cubes (about 2-1/2 cups) (I most often use Yukon gold but any other waxy potato is fine.)

3 egg whites

2 whole eggs

2 tablespoons canola or other vegetable oil

Salt to taste

Method

1. Peel the potatoes and cut into half-inch cubes. Set aside.

2. Fill a large pot with water and bring it to a boil, and then add the potato cubes and cook for 5 minutes. By that time they should be partially cooked. Take a cube out and test it, cutting into it to make sure it is still somewhat firm in the center. If it is too hard, let it cook for another minute. Drain in a colander.

3. In a 12-inch skillet, preferably nonstick, heat the oil over medium heat. Add the potatoes and let them heat through.

Papas con huevo.

4. Crack the egg and egg whites in a bowl, add the salt, and scramble them slightly. Add them to the potatoes, stirring to combine well, and cook until fully cooked, firm but still moist. Add salt according to your taste.

I serve these with hot, wheat flour tortillas and a robust salsa like Chile de Arbol Salsa (page 79). Of course, they invariably will be formed into a taco, the way God intended.

Huevos en Chile Serrano y Tomate | Eggs in Serrano Chile and Tomato

Recipe (serves 4)

These breakfast eggs are immersed and poached in fresh serrano chiles and tomatoes.

My brother, Jimmy, taught me how to make these. He is a master artist in the kitchen and he will probably be peeved when he learns that I have revealed the generous habit he has of traveling to our homes when one of us is sick to make us breakfast. He makes healing, delicious breakfasts and this is one of them. He learned the recipe from our *amá*, Dominga Mora Medrano, who made these for us on weekends. The dish relies on a technique that involves a combination of par-frying and poaching, a method that gives eggs a quick solid form and also tender texture.

Ingredients

1/2 cup white onion, thinly sliced
3 serrano chiles, sliced
1-1/2 cups tomatoes, finely diced
1/2 teaspoon salt
1 tablespoon canola oil
2 cups water
4 eggs
Additional oil as needed for frying the eggs

Method

1. Place the chile and salt in a *molcajete* and mash into a paste. Set aside.
2. In a large deep skillet, sauté the onions in the canola oil until translucent, about 3 minutes. Add the diced tomatoes and continue cooking on low heat for 2 minutes.
3. Add some of the water to the molcajete to help scrape the paste from the sides and add the paste to the onions and tomatoes. Add the remaining water and bring to a simmer. The flavors develop quickly into a delicious sauce akin to *salsa ranchera*. Keep the sauce at a simmer and do not boil.
4. In a nonstick frying pan add just enough oil to cover the bottom.
5. Add each egg, one by one, and fry just to the point where the bottom of the egg begins to turn white. Then gently slide the egg into the chile and tomato sauce and spoon some of the sauce over the egg.
6. When all the eggs are immersed in the sauce, continue gently spooning some of the sauce over the egg yolks to cook them. Keep the sauce at a very slight simmer and cook until the eggs are done to your liking.

Serve the eggs with wheat flour tortillas.

Huevos en chile serrano y tomate.

Huevos en Chile Verde | Eggs with Serrano Chile Sauce

Recipe (serves 4)

This breakfast dish uses two techniques, partially frying (gives form to the eggs) and then poaching in a chile broth (renders the eggs moist and exquisitely flavorful). It's amazing how such a simple, straightforward combination of ingredients makes for such a bright dish. My brother, Jimmy, taught me this recipe and reminds me that our *amá* created the dish. I am glad he paid close attention when she made these.

Ingredients

3 serrano chiles sliced
1/2 teaspoon salt
1 tablespoon canola oil
3 eggs
1/2 cup water

Method

1. In a *molcajete* grind the chile and salt into a paste, add the water, and mix thoroughly.
2. Heat the canola oil in a skillet at medium heat, add the eggs, and scramble vigorously to combine—just a few seconds. As they begin to set, add the chile and water from the molcajete.
3. Bring to a boil and simmer until most of the water has evaporated, stirring from time to time.

Serve immediately. I most often serve these zesty, delicious breakfast eggs with refried beans and wheat flour tortillas.

Huevos Rancheros

Recipe (serves 1)

Ingredients

2 eggs
1/2 cup *salsa ranchera* (recipe on page 81)
1 small waxy potato, peeled and cut into small wedges
1 quart water
2 tablespoons canola or other vegetable oil
1/2 cup refried beans, heated through (recipe on page 45)

Method

1. Peel and cut the potatoes into small wedges.
2. In a saucepan, bring the water to a boil and then add the potatoes, cook at a simmer for 7–9 minutes or until the potato wedges have softened but are still a little resistant when pierced with a toothpick or fork. They will cook completely during the next step.
3. Drain the potatoes, and then add them to a skillet where you have heated 1 tablespoon canola oil over medium heat. Let them cook for 3–5 minutes to allow them to get a little crispy and develop a golden color. Set aside.
4. Heat the salsa ranchera in a small pan and set aside.
5. In a nonstick skillet, heat 1 tablespoon canola oil over medium heat. Gently add the two eggs and cook slowly. If you like them sunny side up, just let them cook a bit. But I like them cooked more, so when the white is cooked, flip the eggs over using

Huevos rancheros.

a rubber spatula. With practice you will not need a spatula; you will just flip them in the pan. Cook the eggs as you like them.

6. Place the eggs on a plate, along with the potatoes and the hot beans. Pour the hot salsa ranchera over the eggs.

Serve immediately with corn or wheat tortillas.

Machacado con Huevo |
Dried, Pounded Beef with Egg
Recipe (serves 4)

Even my niece, Christine Ortega, remembers seeing my father, Juan, and oldest brother, Raúl, construct a small hut using corrugated sheet metal for the walls and roof. They would then salt and string up layers of venison or beef inside the hut, a box really, and let it dry over a period of days. It was delicious beef jerky and from that came the *machacado* used in *machacado con huevo*. Although you can buy machacado at the grocery store, you may want to make it yourself, as I do, using a small dehydrator.

We didn't have dehydrators or corrugated sheet metal four thousand years ago but salting and drying meat was a standard culinary practice. It is not only practical because it preserves meat without refrigeration, it is also tasty.

Ingredients
4 eggs, beaten
2-1/2 ounces *machacado*, Mexican dried beef (2/3 cup) (Buy it from the store or make your own, as described below.)
3 tablespoons white onion, small dice
2/3 cup tomato, diced
2 tablespoons canola oil
1 serrano chile, minced (4 teaspoons)

Method
For the Machacado
To dry the meat, plan ahead. It takes 4–12 hours.

1. Select a cut of meat that has very little fat, such as round steak, shoulder, or rump, and cut it into 1/4-inch to 1/8-inch slices. If the meat is too soft to slice, place it in the freezer for a couple of hours to stiffen it. Slice it lengthwise with the grain so that you see the muscle fibers running up and down, not sideways. By cutting the slices this way you will be able to break the meat into fibrous strands once it is dry.

2. Cover the slices with a very thin layer of fine salt and then follow the instructions for your dehydrator. It will take 4–12 hours.

3. When the meat is dehydrated, use a mallet to pound it and break it apart into thin strands. You thus have machacado.

To Make Machacado con Huevo
Make sure the dried beef is pounded into very small pieces. If the pieces are too large, place them in a *molcajete* and use the *tejolote* to pound them apart into small bits.

1. Heat the canola oil in a skillet over medium heat and add the onion and chile. Cook for 1 minute until the onion softens, and then add the machacado and cook for 2 minutes until the meat is a little crispy.

2. Add the diced tomato and cook, stirring, until it is soft. Then add the beaten eggs and cook on low heat until the egg is done.

Serve it with flour tortillas and refried beans, and thank your maker that our ancestors taught us how to dry meat.

Migas con Chile | Tortilla Crumbs with Scrambled Eggs and Salsa

Recipe (serves 2)

Migas is a traditional Texas Mexican breakfast. I'd like to see more kitchens preparing it because it is delicious, nutritious, and zesty.

"Migas" means crumbs and it refers to the pieces of corn tortillas that are used to make the dish. Many cultures have developed their own crumb dishes, such as, for example, the Spanish with their version of *migas* and Italians with *panzanella*. Ours is quick for breakfast and, with fresh salsa, nutritious. I grew up eating migas this way. Note that there is no cheese, cilantro, oregano, or cumin. Who needs that for breakfast?

Ingredients

4 eggs (You can do what I do and discard two of the yolks to reduce fat and cholesterol.)
4 corn tortillas
1 tablespoon canola oil
Salt to taste

For the Salsa de Chile Verde con Tomate
1 chile serrano, sliced
3/4 cup diced tomato
1/8 teaspoon salt

Migas con chile.

Method

To Make the Salsa

1. Place the salt and serrano chile in a *molcajete* and grind to a fine paste.
2. Add the diced tomato and smash to blend well. Adjust the salt.

To Make the Migas

3. Heat a *comal* or griddle on medium heat and roast the tortillas to the point of golden and crispy, about 5 minutes. Turn them several times.
4. While the tortillas are roasting, heat the canola oil in a nonstick skillet on medium heat. When the oil is hot but not smoking, crumble the tortillas onto the skillet and toss for 5 seconds to coat.
5. Lower the heat to low, add the eggs, and scramble until all the tortilla pieces are coated with egg. Sprinkle with salt. Cook the eggs through but without drying them.

To serve, spoon a generous ribbon of the salsa on the *migas*. Enjoy with a hot cup of *café de olla*, and then go out and make this a better world.

Nopalitos con Huevo | Cactus with Scrambled Eggs

Recipe (serves 1)

Served with freshly made corn tortillas, the tang and crispness of the *nopalitos* is wonderful with eggs for breakfast. This is such an obvious combination if you are living in the Texas Mexican triangle and look out to see a cactus and an egg.

It was a wise and observant cook who first invented this combination.

Ingredients

1/2 cup *nopales* (cactus paddles) cut into 1/2-inch squares (This dish must be made with fresh nopalitos. Every time that I tested prepackaged nopalitos, the taste was so awful I've had to spit them out. When you buy the fresh cactus, it will have spines, some very tiny, and even powdery. To remove the spines, I place the cactus paddles on sheets of newspaper and, holding each with tongs, scrape away the spines with a potato peeler. After you do this a couple of times, you will learn how not to get spines all over your arms. A shop near my home sells fresh nopalitos and two highly skilled ladies will clean them for you on the spot.)

1 egg
1 egg white
1 tablespoon canola or other vegetable oil
Salt to taste

Method

1. Heat the canola oil in a skillet at medium heat. Add the *nopal* squares and sauté for 13 minutes. They will acquire a nice color and the viscous juices will evaporate.
2. Add the egg, egg white, and salt, and scramble continuously until the cactus squares are coated with the eggs. Cook for about 2 minutes until the eggs are cooked, but not dry. Adjust the salt.

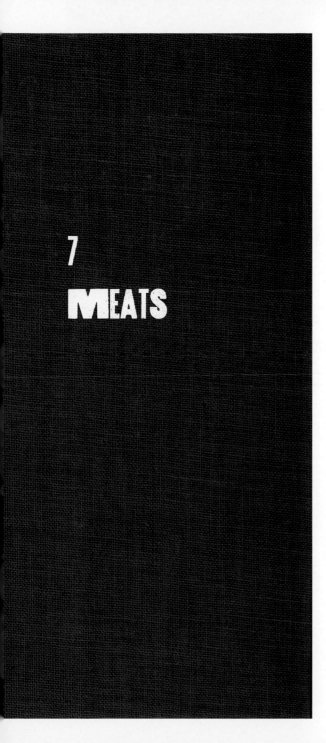

7

MEATS

Albóndigas de Chile Ancho |
Ancho Chile Meatballs

Recipe (makes 40 1-1/2-inch albóndigas)

Albóndigas illustrate the dynamism of food pathways, the routes by which foods travel via bird flights, human wars, marriages, and so on. As it travels, food changes, rcfashioning itself into new cultural types. This Texas Mexican meatball, albóndiga, originally comes to us from the Spaniards who arrived in the 1500s. "Albóndiga," an Arab word, settled into Spanish cuisine because, of course, Spain was an Arab territory from 711 until 1492 when the Arabs were expelled militarily from the Iberian Peninsula.

The flavoring for this meatball is *chile ancho*, although *chipotle* is most commonly used in albóndigas throughout our region. I like the taste of the ancho because it reminds me of *carne con chile*. The rest of the recipe is straight from the Arabic Morocco, Spanish method: bread and eggs. Three native ingredients transform this Arab dish into Texas Mexican: Mexican oregano, chile ancho, and tomatoes.

Albóndigas de chile ancho.

Ingredients

For the Adobo
4 ancho chiles, seeded and deveined
1 white onion
3 garlic cloves
2 teaspoons fresh Mexican oregano
1 teaspoon salt
1 tablespoon canola oil
2 cups tomatoes, diced
2 cups chicken stock
1/4 teaspoon sugar
1/2 tablespoon white vinegar

For the Meatballs
1 pound ground pork
1 pound 96% fat-free ground beef
1 egg, beaten
2 teaspoons salt
3 ounces bread slices, crust removed, broken up
    into 1-inch pieces (about 1-1/2 cups or 3 slices)
1/2 cup milk

Method

To Make the Chile Purée and Meatballs
Preheat the oven to 400°F.

1. Remove the seeds from the chiles by cutting a slit lengthwise in each chile to open it and remove the stem with the attached seeds. Remove all the other seeds in the chile pod.

2. Place the chiles in a large pot and cover them with water. Bring to a boil, turn off the heat, and let the chiles steep for 15 minutes so that they will rehydrate. Drain and allow to cool. Discard the water.

3. Place the chiles, onion, garlic, oregano, and salt in a blender. Add 1 cup of clean water and blend on high until the paste is completely smooth, with no large particles. Add a little more water if needed. If there are large particles in the paste after you are done blending, strain the paste through a fine-mesh sieve. Set aside.

4. Heat the canola oil in a Dutch oven and add the chile purée, with caution because there will be splatter as the liquid meets the oil. Fry for 10 minutes. The color will deepen and the purée will thicken. Set aside.

5. In a bowl, pour the milk, add the bread, and set aside.

6. Mix together the pork and beef.

7. Add the beaten egg to the meat. Squeeze excess milk from the bread and mix it with the meat using your hands or a large spatula or spoon.

8. Add 8 tablespoons of the ancho chile puréc to the meat and mix thoroughly.

9. Form the seasoned meat into 40 1-1/2-inch balls and place them on a large cookie sheet.

10. Roast the meatballs in a 400°F oven for 12–15 minutes until browned and crispy on the outside. Remove from the oven and allow the meatballs to rest for 10 minutes. They are ready to serve with the *adobo*.

To Make the Adobo

11. To the remaining chile purée add the tomatoes, chicken stock, and sugar and bring to a boil. Cook for 30 minutes until the adobo begins to thicken. Taste and correct the salt.

Serve the meatballs on a plate and pour the adobo over

them. Or you can serve the *adobo* on the side, with toothpicks for each guest to dip.

These *albóndigas* are moist and delicious even on the second day and will keep in the fridge for 5 days.

Arroz con Pollo | Rice with Chicken
Recipe (serves 8)

A whole chicken, cut up into parts, was what went into this iconic "familia" dish for us Texas Mexicans, Mexicanos, Mexican Americans, Chicanos. We were also called *pochos* by some, and "greasers" by others. I grew up with all these names surrounding me, some in English, some in Spanish, all the while nourished by this dish and enjoying it immensely. My *amá* made it regularly, browning the chicken, rocking spices in the *molcajete*, filling the kitchen with flavor-some aromas.

The two languages of conquest, English and Spanish, moved around me from label to label but our food remained our own creation. Some of the flavoring ingredients are originally from Asia, Africa, and the Mediterranean, brought here by Europeans: rice, black pepper, garlic, and cumin. But as I cook the dish in my kitchen, I find the sense of it to be indigenous. The tomato and chile provide the dominant flavor theme in the profile. They harmoniously envelop all the ingredients, giving the dish the taste that identifies it as ours. The techniques employed in cooking this dish are a continuation of the techniques used since our earliest days on this land: grinding, blending, boiling, and perking it up with some fat. Knowing my mother, I can easily see someone like her using these same techniques 600 or 2,000 years ago to make a stew that would have, and did, combine a bird with judicious use of grain, roots, spices, tomatoes, chiles, and some fat.

Ingredients
3 pounds chicken, cut up into parts
2 tablespoons canola oil
2 cups rice
1 garlic clove
1/4 teaspoon black peppercorns
1/4 teaspoon cumin
1/4 cup water
4 tomatoes, diced (about 3/4 pound)
1 white onion, thin slices
1 green *chile dulce* (bell pepper), 1/4-inch–1/2-inch wide slices
1/2 teaspoon salt
4 cups water

Method
1. Place the garlic, cumin, and black pepper in the *molcajete* and grind into a paste. Add 1/4 cup water and mix. Set aside.
2. In a large skillet or Dutch oven, heat the canola oil and brown the chicken in batches. Place the browned chicken on paper towels. Remove all but 2 tablespoons of the fat from the pan.
3. Add the rice, onion, and chile dulce, and cook for 5 minutes. Then add the browned chicken, tomatoes, salt, the molcajete paste, and 4 cups water. Mix so that the ingredients are combined, scraping the bottom to remove browned bits. Bring to a boil, reduce the heat to low and simmer, covered, for 30 minutes.

This is a classic Texas Mexican dish that says "wholesome, delicious."

Puerco en Chile Colorado | Pork in Red Chile
Recipe (serves 4)

This is another of the iconic Texas Mexican dishes that is shared with other regions, especially the northern regions of Mexico, with each region having its own variations. I grew up with this on our table, whenever we could afford meat, and to this day I just love the aroma and invigorating flavors of the red chiles with the roasted vegetables and spices. The guajillo chile is prized for its deep red color.

Seasoning meats with variously flavored chiles and roasting tomatoes and roots were already a Texas Indian culinary technique before pork arrived. I celebrate how the Texas Indian cooks went on to develop new and brilliant dishes after 1500, when European immigrants stepped ashore, bringing with them pigs, onions, garlic, black pepper, and cumin. This dish has its Texas roots certainly somewhere in the seventeenth century (Berzok, 2005) and celebrates indigenous (*indio*) identity. It emphasizes to me, as a culinarian, how we may encounter "otherness" in life-giving rather than war-making ways. The culinary arts open up an aesthetic of welcoming.

Ingredients
- 1 pound pork loin, trimmed of fat and cut into 1/2-inch cubes
- 4 guajillo chiles, dried, deseeded, and deveined

Puerco en chile colorado.

1/2 teaspoon cumin seeds

3 Roma tomatoes

1 small white onion, peeled

1/2 teaspoon black peppercorns

1 garlic clove, unpeeled

1 teaspoon fresh Mexican oregano

1/4 teaspoon salt

2 tablespoons canola or other vegetable oil

2-1/2 cups water

Method

1. In a cast-iron skillet or griddle (no oil added), dry roast the tomatoes, onion, and unpeeled garlic on medium heat until they develop black spots. Peel the garlic after roasting. Set aside to cool.

2. Remove the seeds from the chiles by cutting a slit lengthwise in each chile to open it and remove the stem with the attached seeds. Remove all other seeds in the chile pod.

3. Place the chiles in a large pot and cover them with water. Bring to a boil, turn off the heat, and let the chiles steep for 15 minutes so that they will rehydrate. Drain and allow to cool. Discard the water.

4. Place the chiles, roasted vegetables, spices, and salt in a blender and blend to a fine paste. Add 1/2–1 cup additional fresh water as needed to keep the ingredients blending properly. If there are large particles in the paste after you have finished blending, strain the paste through a fine-mesh sieve. Set aside.

5. In a Dutch oven heat the canola oil and then add the pork cubes in small batches to brown them. You don't want to add the cubes all at once because crowding them in the Dutch oven will make them sweat and release their juices. You want to only brown them. Set aside the browned pork.

6. In the same Dutch oven add the chile and vegetable purée (be careful because it will splatter as you pour) and cook for 8–10 minutes, scraping the bottom to release any dark bits, until most of the liquid has evaporated. You will see the color deepen.

7. Return the pork to the Dutch oven and add 2 cups of water. Bring to a boil and then turn down the heat and simmer, covered, for 30 minutes until the pork is fully cooked and tender. Uncover and cook a bit more, about 10 minutes, until the liquid has reduced and the chile has thickened. Taste and adjust the salt.

Serve this beautiful dish with rice and hot, toasty corn tortillas.

Barbacoa al Horno | Braised Beef for Barbacoa Tacos

Recipe (makes tacos for 8)

Earth ovens are ancient and found all over the globe. This seems to be an instinctive cooking technique that we share as humans. In San Antonio, where there is evidence of human habitation dating back 13,000 years, archaeologists have found layers of heated rocks suggesting that it was part of an earth oven (a pit) built 4,500 years ago (Black and Dial, 2006). The archaeological site is called Olmos Dam because the dam is nearby.

Eight miles southwest of Olmos Dam, my father continued this ancient tradition. He would build an earthen oven pit, 3 feet by 3 feet, in our backyard on

Barbacoa al horno.

the west side of San Antonio. Alongside the pit, and accompanied by my uncles and *compadres*, he would build a very large wood fire that would eventually turn into a huge pile of coals. While the fire was burning he would prepare a cow head, sometimes a goat or other meat, by wrapping it tightly in burlap. It was at this time that my mother would appear from the house with a bowl of spices, blended with water, and throw them into the burlap as the meat was being wrapped.

My father shoveled half the coals into the bottom of the pit and placed the burlapped meat on top of them. Again, thankfully, my mother intervened, and with a flourish threw in a bowl of liquefied spices onto the top of the burlap bag. The men shoveled the rest of the coals on top of that, laid a metal sheet over the pit, and then covered everything with dirt. There was a pipe sticking out of the hole.

Eight to 12 hours later the pit was dug up and we enjoyed the most flavorful, moist, delectable *barbacoa* in the world. It was amazing.

This was during my childhood and continued until the 1990s when *apá* passed away. Today I don't have any space in my backyard to build a pit, so this recipe is intended for the indoor home oven. I don't use a cow's head or beef cheeks, which are the requisite for *barbacoa*. If you want to taste delicious authenticity, use beef cheeks instead of the roast I recommend in the recipe. Either way, the result is evocative of the taste I remember, albeit with no smoke. The spices are those my mom used, as best I can determine by checking with my family. I hope you enjoy it, especially with your loved ones. We continue a 4,000-year tradition of savory slow cooking.

Ingredients

 2 pounds boneless beef chuck
 3 garlic cloves, peeled and crushed
 1/2 white onion
 1/2 teaspoon black peppercorns, crushed
 1/2 teaspoon salt
 2 2-inch sprigs of fresh Texas Mexican oregano
  (1/4 teaspoon dry)

Method

Preheat oven to 200°F.

1. Place the beef in a Dutch oven and fill it halfway with water. Add the crushed garlic, onion, black peppercorns, and oregano, and bring to a boil. Turn off the heat.

2. Cover tightly, place in a 200°F oven and cook for 6–8 hours. Turn the meat over once during cooking.

3. When the beef is done, place it on a cutting board or large bowl and, using forks or wooden spoons, pull the meat apart. Adjust the salt. Keep the meat warm for making individual tacos.

To make the tacos, serve it with hot corn tortillas, an array of salsas, fresh coarsely chopped cilantro, and Mexican lime wedges. An abrupt conversation hiatus, with groans of satisfaction, will ensue.

Calabacita con Pollo Herbido | Chicken Poached in Cumin Garlic Broth

Recipe (serves 6)

In this recipe I twist a classic Texas Mexican dish, *calabacita con pollo*, by poaching rather than frying. I like an ongoing culinary dialog between us and regions south of us. Why change tradition?

Calabacita con pollo herbido.

Hidalgo, in the central eastern region of Mexico, is the homeland of the great Toltec culture. Toltec art and huge monuments are among the best known in Meso-america, but a lesser-known fact is that the region has a delicious, distinctive cuisine. *Gallina en ajo comino* is a Hidalgo dish that uses poaching as a method for infusing flavors into food as it cooks with no fat. The French have a similar method, known as *court bouillon*, which is used to deep-poach foods.

I use the Hidalgo cooking method to make our traditional *calabacita con pollo*. I hope you will agree that it is delicious and just right for company.

Ingredients

2-1/2 pounds chicken, skinned, trimmed of all fat, cut into 1–2-inch pieces

1 tablespoon garlic, minced

1/4 teaspoon ground cumin

3 cups water

1 teaspoon salt

1 tablespoon canola oil

1-1/2 cup tomatoes, small dice

1 white onion, sliced

1 tablespoon serrano chile, sliced into circles

2 large Mexican tatuma squash (*calabacita*) 1/4-inch round slices (You can substitute zucchini if tatuma is not available.)

Method

1. Place the water, garlic, and cumin in a large skillet or sauté pan and bring to the boiling point. Add the chicken pieces and keep the fire on high to bring the liquid back to just barely a low simmer. Lower the heat and keep poaching at a very low simmer until the chicken is fully cooked, approximately 20 minutes. Remove the chicken and hold warm. Strain the liquid with a fine-mesh sieve and hold.

2. In a Dutch oven or deep skillet heat the canola oil. Add the onions and cook until they are soft and translucent.

3. While the onions are cooking, grind the serrano chile and the salt into a fine paste using a *molcajete*. Add a little of the strained broth to the molcajete to lift off the paste and add it to the onions.

4. Add the tomatoes, 1-1/2 cups of the strained broth and cook this sauce, uncovered, on medium heat for 15 minutes.

5. Add the chicken pieces and continue cooking until the chicken is heated through.

6. Add the calabacita on top, cover and simmer for 7–10 minutes until the calabacita is cooked but not mushy. Adjust the salt.

Serve the chicken with hot corn tortillas.

Caldo de Res | Beef Soup
Recipe (serves 6)

This is a dish that brings warmth, on many levels, such as appreciation for the bounty of the land and as a catalyst of intimate family dissension. Some of us wanted *amá* to add chile serrano to the soup, but others mightily said "no way!"

Ingredients

1-1/2 pounds beef shank with bone

1 pound beef chuck, cut in large cubes

3 quarts water

2 tablespoons salt

1/2 tablespoons ground black pepper

1 turnip, peeled and cut into 2-inch pieces

1/4 cabbage, cut into 2-inch pieces

1/2 *chile dulce* (bell pepper) , cut into 2-inch strips

2 carrots, peeled and cut into 2-inch pieces

2 medium potatoes, peeled and cut into 2-inch pieces

4 green onions, washed and root ends sliced off

1/2 white onion cut into 2-inch pieces

2 ears of corn, each cut into 3 or 4 pieces

1 or 2 serrano chiles (optional), whole and removed from the soup before serving (Save the cooked chiles to make salsa another time.)

Method

1. In a large pot, add the meat and water and bring to a boil. Reduce the heat and simmer for 1 or 2 hours, until the meat is tender. With a large spoon or ladle, skim off and discard all the foam that forms on the top.

2. Add the vegetables, salt, and pepper, and cook for another 20 minutes. Add the corn at the last 10 minutes so it will be just tender and plump. Correct the salt before serving.

Accompany the soup with lots of chopped cilantro and lime wedges.

Carne Guisada con Papas | Beef Stewed with Potatoes
Recipe (serves 6)

Chile is Mexican and the scientific name is *Capsicum*. Pepper is Indian (India) and the scientific name is *Piper*. I find it interesting how language constantly changes. When our European ancestors, searching for India, landed instead in the Caribbean and South America, they called the South American natives "Indians." Upon finding chiles, they used the spicy default name with which they were familiar, "pepper."

This recipe uses both chile and pepper, ground in a *molcajete* together with garlic and cumin. A stewed beef dish, it is aromatic and its flavor profile is wonderfully contrasted between black pepper and *chile serrano*. The flavor profile of a dish consists of the identifiable taste, odor, mouth feel, and aftertaste. In my opinion, achieving the correct flavor profile for *carne guisada* depends entirely on what you grind in your molcajete, that is, the mixture of ingredients to include cumin, garlic, and both pepper and chile. Note the use of wheat flour as a thickener.

Ingredients

1-1/2 pounds round steak, trimmed of fat and cut into 1/2-inch cubes

2 waxy potatoes, 14 ounces, cut into 1/2-inch cubes

1 large white onion, sliced

2 tablespoons canola oil

1/2 tablespoon all-purpose flour

2-1/2 cups water, approximately

1 serrano chile, sliced

15 black peppercorns
2 garlic cloves, peeled and sliced
1/4 teaspoon cumin seeds
1 teaspoon salt

Method

1. Heat 1 tablespoon canola oil in a Dutch oven, medium heat, and brown the meat for about a minute. Do this in batches if necessary so that the meat will not be crowded.
2. Add the onions to the meat in the Dutch oven and cook until translucent, about 2 minutes.
3. In a *molcajete*, grind the chiles, pepper, garlic, cumin, and salt to achieve a very fine paste. Add it to the meat and onions. Do this by adding a little water to the molcajete, allowing you to scrape the paste away from the molcajete. You may have to do this a couple of times to get all the paste.
4. Dissolve the flour in 2-1/2 cups water and add it to the meat and deglaze, scraping the bottom to unstick browned bits. The water should just cover the meat, so adjust accordingly. Bring to a boil, and then lower the heat and simmer at slightly below a full boil, about 200°F, covered, for 30 minutes and up to 2 hours. At this low heat the beef collagen changes into gelatin and renders the beef both soft and flavorful. If the heat is too high, the beef will be tough. Didn't you learn this from your "stone-boiling" archaeology class?
5. Remove the cover during the last 10 minutes, add the potatoes, and continue cooking. The sauce will thicken. Taste and adjust the salt.

Serve *carne guisada* with hot corn or wheat flour tortillas.

Carnitas | Pork Tips

Recipe (serves 8)

These crispy-outside, moist-inside little pork chunks are for snacking and for making tacos with friends. Simple and straightforward is simply good.

Ingredients

3 pounds pork, cut into 2-inch cubes (This can be shoulder chuck, country-style ribs, or a combination of both.)
1/2 white onion
2 garlic cloves
1/4 teaspoon salt, or to taste
1 bay leaf
1-1/2 cups water
2 tablespoons peanut oil or lard

Method

1. Place the pork in a Dutch oven, cast iron if available, and add the water and all the ingredients except the oil. Cover and simmer for 1 hour. Then uncover and cook on medium until all the water has evaporated.
2. Add the oil and continue to cook, frying for 30–45 minutes, and turning the meat so that it turns golden and crisp.

Make tacos with either wheat flour or corn tortillas and accentuate with *salsa verde cocida* or another salsa and fresh cilantro.

Carne con Chile a.k.a. Chile con Carne
Recipe (serves 6)

Here in Texas everybody and her/his cow has the authentic Texas "chili" recipe. Yup, replete with that "secret ingredient" and those implausible anecdotes about a cow falling into a vat of chiles, a deer getting stewed by mistake 'cause my cousin was drunk, etcetera and so on.

Carne con chile means "meat with chile." We never used the term, "*chile con carne.*" However, now the two terms are interchangeable for this stew that at times just feels like the perfect food for body and soul. This recipe is one I hope you will like. I use chile *ancho* as the base, *guajillo* for red color, and *chipotle* for a nice tang. The other seasonings are a classic Texas Mexican combination that I think blends perfectly such that you don't have one flavor springing up over any other.

"Chili" is the anglicized word for chile. Non-Spanish Texans who migrated from Europe fell in love with the various native Mexican dishes, all made with creative combinations of chiles. In San Antonio, for example, open-air food stands, a native tradition dating back to the 1300s, served a wide array of indigenous foods: enchiladas, tamales, tortillas, and a stew of meat with chile, carne con chile. All of these dishes used chiles as the base flavoring, but it seems that "chili" was easier for the newly arrived to pronounce so it stuck as the popular term. Now the word is used as the proper name of the traditional dish, carne con chile a.k.a. chile con carne. So let's get down and make some "chili." Sometimes I make it with venison and sometimes with beef, although never together. Both beef and venison versions are delicious.

Ingredients
4 ancho chiles, seeded and deveined
2 guajillo chiles, seeded and deveined
1 chipotle chile, seeded and deveined
2 garlic cloves, unpeeled
1 medium white onion, peeled
1/2 teaspoon powdered cumin
1 teaspoon fresh Mexican oregano
2 teaspoons salt
2 tablespoons canola oil
2 pounds beef-chuck shoulder roast, or venison, cut into 1-inch cubes
3 cups water

Method
1. In a large skillet, heat 1 tablespoon canola oil and brown the meat cubes. If necessary do this in batches so that the meat is not crowded in the skillet. Set aside and keep warm.
2. To devein the chiles, first lay the chile flat on a cutting board and, using a paring knife, cut a slit lengthwise. Then grab the chile with one hand and with the other break off the stem. Open the chile along the slit and remove the seeds and veins.
3. In a large saucepan, cover the cleaned chiles with water and bring to a boil. Turn off the heat and let the chiles steep for 15 minutes so that they rehydrate and become tender. Drain the chiles, discarding the water. Set aside to cool.
4. Heat a *comal* or a cast-iron skillet on high, and then roast (i.e., no oil) the onion and the garlic until the onion has softened and has black spots. Peel the garlic after it has cooked and become soft.

Carne con chile a.k.a. *chile con carne.*

5. Place the onion, garlic, chiles, cumin, oregano, and salt in a blender, and blend to a very fine paste. To blend well, you will need to add 1/2–1 cup water.

6. In a Dutch oven, heat the canola oil and add the chile paste. There will be splatter, so be prepared for it. Cook for 10 minutes, stirring all the while.

7. Add the browned meat and 3 cups of water and bring to a very slow simmer. By this I mean that you'll see only small, slow bubbles on the surface. Cover and cook for 2 hours, all the while adjusting the heat so that it stays at a slow simmer and does not boil. Uncover and cook for another 30 minutes or so to thicken. Adjust the salt.

I often use a crockpot set at medium or high, after adding the meat (step 7), and slow cook it for 6–8 hours. It turns out delicious.

Serve the chile con carne immediately or the next day with a garnish of diced white onion, cheddar cheese, and diced, pickled jalapeños. Make sure you make plenty because it will also taste fantastic the following day.

Chilorio | Pulled Pork in Chile
Recipe (serves 6)

Chilorio is a specialty of Sinaloa, Mexico, and resembles our Texas Mexican *carne con chile*. Alston V. Thoms writes, "Given substantial populations in all parts of Texas for thousands of years, it is unlikely that there were any significant trade secrets in the world of basic cooking technology. In summary, the people of the interior South Texas were surely familiar with the types of game animals, aquatic resources and plant foods found in adjacent regions as well as with the methods the people there used to procure, process, cook and consume those resources" (Thoms, 2012).

Chilorio is a type of pulled pork that is cooked by boiling, a technique that dates back thousands of years. The cooking implement was made by digging a bowl in the earth, covering it with bark or hide, and adding hot stones to bring the water to a boil. As the meat cooked slowly, it became "fall-apart" tender. This technique, called stone-boiling, was employed by the indigenous people of what is now Texas and northern Mexico. They traveled back and forth across regions so it is not surprising that the chilorio, pulled pork of Sinaloa, is similar to our *carne con chile*. Alex Krieger studied the route that Cabeza de Vaca followed in the 1500s and he draws the route going from Galveston to Mexico City via the entire north-to-south length of the Mexican state of Sinaloa, home of chilorio (Krieger, 2002).

There were other similar travel routes that made it commonplace for cooks in neighboring regions to exchange techniques and ideas.

Ingredients
1-1/2 pounds pork shoulder, cut into 1-inch or 2-inch cubes
1/2 teaspoon salt
1/3 cup canola oil
4 ancho chiles, wiped clean, seeded and deveined
1 pasilla chile, wiped clean, seeded and deveined
3 garlic cloves
1/2 teaspoon coriander seeds
1/2 teaspoon cumin seeds
1/2 teaspoon dried oregano

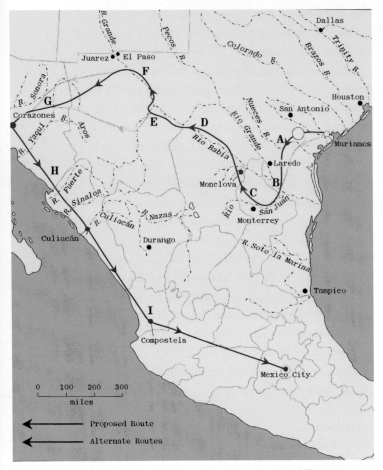

Route of Cabeza de Vaca from Galveston Island, Texas, to Mexico City. Reprinted with permission from Alex D. Krieger, *We Came Naked and Barefoot: The Journey of Cabeza de Vaca across North America*, edited by Margery H. Krieger (Austin: University of Texas Press, 2002). Alterations based on map from *Texas Beyond History*, Texas Archeological Research Laboratory, University of Texas at Austin.

1/8 teaspoon black peppercorns
1 tablespoon white vinegar
1 tablespoon rice vinegar

Method

1. In a saucepan, place the pork cubes and add water to cover them, add the salt, and bring to a boil. Lower the heat and simmer covered until the pork is fully cooked and soft, about 1 hour. Uncover in the last 15 minutes so that most of the water will evaporate.

2. Transfer the pork to a cutting board or large bowl and pull apart the meat strands using two large spoons or spatulas. Set aside.

3. Using a *comal* or cast-iron skillet, dry roast the chiles slightly, rather than charring them. Place the roasted chiles in a bowl of hot water and let them soak for 15 minutes to rehydrate and soften. Discard the water.

4. In a blender, place the rehydrated chiles, garlic, 1/2 cup of fresh water, and all the spices and vinegars. Blend on high until you have an extremely smooth purée.

5. In a Dutch oven heat the canola oil, and when it is shimmering add the chile purée. There will be splatter so be careful. Fry the purée for 5–8 minutes or until the color deepens and it thickens.

6. Add the meat to the chile, combine well, and cook for 15 minutes until the pork is heated through. Taste and adjust the salt.

Serve and enjoy with warm wheat flour tortillas.

Recipes

Tacos de Chorizo con Papas | Mexican Chorizo with Potato Tacos

Recipe (serves 4)

Ingredients

4 ounces *chorizo* (3/4 c)

1 tablespoon canola or other vegetable oil (Omit this oil if the *chorizo* you are using has a lot of fat.)

1 medium waxy potato, cut into 1/4-inch cubes (about 1 cup)

1 tablespoon *jalapeños en escabeche* (pickled jalapeños), finely minced

1 ounce Chihuahua cheese (*queso chihuahua*), cut into 8 thin strips or small cubes for easy melting. (Named after the Mexican state where it was first made, this is a mild but flavorful cheese. It is creamy, velvety, and melts easily.)

8 corn tortillas

1/8 teaspoon salt

Method

1. If using the oil, heat it over medium heat in a skillet, preferably nonstick, and cook the chorizo for 10 minutes. If the chorizo has a lot of fat, drain most of it off after the sausage has cooked, leaving about 1 tablespoon.
2. Add the potato cubes and salt; mix together. Lower the heat, cover tightly, and cook for 10 minutes or until the potatoes are cooked. Uncover and cook an additional 4 minutes to evaporate some of the liquid.
3. Add the minced pickled jalapeño. Then set the mixture aside and keep it warm.
4. Heat the corn tortillas and divide the chorizo mixture and the cheese among them, making sumptuous, decadent tacos.

Fajitas

Recipe (serves 8)

Backyard grilling is spelled *fajitas* in Mexican American homes. *Fajita* means little belt and it refers to the cut of the meat being from the diaphragm of the cow. The flavor of the skirt is outstanding and it is very tough. Fajitas have become commercially omnipresent, and I think it is because of their sizzle, in this case the sizzle being the superb taste. In this recipe I cook them indoors, on a very hot griddle. Papaya and slicing the skirt thinly overcome the toughness.

Papaya, native to Mexico and Central America, is not only a highly efficient meat tenderizer, but it also matches well with the other flavorings of the marinade. Do not marinate more than 2 hours because the tenderizing enzyme in the papaya, papain, will make the meat too soft.

Ingredients

3 pounds beef skirt meat

2 tablespoons canola or peanut oil

1 cup fresh papaya, diced

1/2 teaspoon salt

For the Marinade

1 cup apple cider vinegar

1/2 cup *piloncillo* (brown sugar may be substituted)

1/2 cup white onion, diced

Meats

Chorizo con papas.

2 teaspoons black pepper

4 garlic cloves, peeled

2 teaspoons salt

Method

1. Place the diced papaya and the salt in a blender and make a fine paste. Pour into a large bowl and set aside.
2. Rinse the blender well, and then add all the marinade ingredients and blend until smooth.
3. Dip the thin skirt meat into the papaya purée and toss to coat all sides with papaya. Shake the meat to remove excess papaya, and then transfer to a glass container.
4. Pour the marinade over the meat, adding a little water if needed to make sure all of the meat is covered. Refrigerate for 1 hour.
5. Heat a griddle or cast-iron skillet to 400°F, brush it with the oil, and cook the meat, browning each side for about 4–5 minutes.

     Let the meat rest for 15 minutes, and then slice it into 1/4-inch thick strips, cutting against the grain. Serve with wheat flour tortillas and salsa. Honestly, my mouth is watering just imagining these tacos.

Guajolote Asado Relleno con Pan de Maíz | Roasted Turkey with Cornbread Stuffing

Recipe (servings depend on the size of the turkey)

This stuffed turkey triggers a unique memory for me: being at home, at the table, among family. It's my *amá's* recipe and she made it every Thanksgiving. What makes it unique and different from any other stuffed turkey I have made is the combination of the turkey, corn, *chile dulce*, and pecans, all native ingredients, with the strong, sweet flavor of raisins.

Guajolotes are native to Mexico and the U.S. Southwest. They were domesticated by our ancestors as early as 2,000 years ago (Speller, Kemp, Lipe, and Yang, 2010). When the Spaniards arrived in Mexico, they found that this large bird formed part of our diet and proceeded to export it to Europe where it acquired its new name, "turkey." Preparing it today sometimes seems like a 2,000-year-old déjà vu.

Ingredients

1 turkey with giblets

1 tablespoon vegetable oil

4 cups water

For Cornbread Dressing (makes 3 quarts)

6 cups cornbread (double the recipe on page 51)

1-1/2 cup white onion, small dice

2/3 cup celery, small dice

1 cup green *chile dulce* (bell pepper), small dice

4 tablespoons canola oil or other vegetable oil

1 cup pecan pieces that have been roasted in a 350°F oven for 8–10 minutes so that they have a nice deep color, but are not burned

1/2 cup black raisins

2 cups broth from boiling the turkey giblets

1/2 teaspoon salt

Method

Preheat the oven to 350°F.

1. Remove the giblets from the turkey and simmer them in 4 cups of water for 1 hour, while skimming and discarding the foam that forms on top.

Meats

2. Make cornbread (page 51) and after it cools, slice a portion that will measure 6 cups when crumbled. Use your fingers or a food processor to crumble the bread. Crumbs should be no larger than the size of a pea. Set aside in a large bowl.

3. In a skillet, heat the oil on medium heat and add the onion, celery, and chile dulce. Cook, stirring, until the vegetables are soft, about 5 minutes.

4. Add the cooked vegetables to the cornbread, along with the roasted pecans, raisins, and salt. Mix thoroughly.

5. Add 1-1/2 cups of the giblet broth to the mixture and mix well with a large spoon or spatula. You may add a little more liquid if the stuffing seems too dry. Taste and adjust the salt.

6. To stuff the turkey, first fill the neck cavity, and then pull the skin over to cover the stuffed cavity and secure it with a toothpick or skewer. Next, stuff the body cavity of the turkey, and also finish by covering the cavity with the skin. Join the two ends of the legs together over the opening and tie with string. You will have plenty of stuffing left over and it can be served separately in a casserole dish.

7. Place the *guajolote* in the 350°F oven. It will take 20 minutes per pound to cook. The turkey is ready when the internal temperature is 165°F. It is important that the temperature be no less than 165°F for safety reasons. If parts of the turkey are brown enough but other parts still need more cooking, try placing aluminum foil on top of the parts that are done to slow the browning.

Place the additional stuffing in a casserole, and bake in a 350°F oven for 30 minutes before serving.

Menudo | Red Chile Tripe Soup
Recipe (serves 8)

Everyone knows that this is the official breakfast you have after a long night of revelry. Many will swear that it is the perfect cure for a hangover. For us it marked Christmas, for there was always a potful on the stove to greet our relatives and friends as they performed their holiday *visita*.

If you have a way of boiling the *menudo* outside on the porch, I recommend that you do so as sometimes the smell of tripe boiling is strong and lingers.

Ingredients
2 pounds honeycomb tripe
7 garlic cloves, peeled and cut in half
1 small white onion, peeled and quartered
1-1/2 gallons water
1 tablespoon salt or to taste
1-1/2 pounds *maíz pozolero* (page 114) or canned hominy

For Accompaniments
3 Mexican limes, cut in wedges
1 white onion, finely diced
1 dozen corn tortillas

For the Chile Paste
2 guajillo chiles, deseeded and deveined
3 ancho chiles, deseeded and deveined
1-1/2 tablespoons dried Mexican oregano
1 teaspoon cumin seeds
3 garlic cloves
1 cup water

Method

1. Wash the tripe thoroughly and cut it into 1-inch squares.
2. Place in a large pot, add 1-1/2 gallons of water, and bring to a boil. Turn down the heat to an energetic boil and cook until tender. Depending on the tripe, cooking could take 3–6 hours. From time to time, skim and discard the foam that forms on the top.

For the Chile Paste

3. To devein the chiles, first lay the chile flat on a cutting board and, using a paring knife, cut a slit lengthwise. Then grab the chile with one hand and with the other break off the stem. Open the chile along the slit and remove the seeds and veins.
4. In a large saucepan, cover the cleaned chiles with water and bring to a boil. Turn off the heat and let the chiles steep for 15 minutes so that they rehydrate and become tender. Drain the chiles, discarding the water. Let the chiles cool a bit so as not to damage your blender.
5. Place the chiles in a blender along with the garlic, cumin, and oregano. Blend to a very fine paste, adding water as needed. You will need to add 1/2–1 cup water.
6. When the menudo is cooked tender, add the chile paste and hominy and cook, uncovered, for another 30 minutes.

Serve with hot corn tortillas, lime wedges, and diced white onion. You'll feel restored.

Picadillo | Ground Beef Stew
Recipe (serves 4)

Texas Mexican *picadillo* is seasoned with black pepper, cumin, and garlic.

We add potatoes but not raisins or olives as is typical farther south and especially in the Caribbean. This is our family recipe and how I make it at home. Flavors are blended so harmoniously that not one spice outshines the other. It is robust and straightforward, like us.

Ingredients

1 pound lean ground beef
1/3 cup white onion, diced
1 tablespoon vegetable oil
1 clove garlic
1 teaspoon salt
8 black peppercorns
1/8 teaspoon cumin seeds
1 large wax potato like Yukon gold, cut into 1-inch cubes (about 2 cups)
3 cups water

Method

1. In a skillet heat the oil on medium heat, and then add the onions and cook until they are soft. Add the ground beef and brown it.
2. While the meat is browning, place the garlic, salt, black peppercorns, and cumin seeds in a *molcajete* and grind into a fine paste. Add the paste to the meat by pouring a little water into the *molcajete* to

scrape away the paste. Then add 3 cups water and scrape the bottom of the skillet to deglaze.

3. Add the potatoes, cover, and cook for 10 minutes. Uncover and continue cooking until most of the liquid evaporates but the stew is still soupy, about 5–10 minutes.

Serve with wheat flour tortillas. Picadillo is always welcome as tacos.

Pozole or Posole

Recipe (serves 8–12)

Pozole cooked with red chiles is also made by native communities northwest of us, the Pueblos in New Mexico and Navajos in Arizona (Keegan, 2010).

For this recipe I boil white, dry corn with slaked lime (calcium hydroxide), a process called nixtamalization, which was invented by indigenous cooks thousands of years ago. Nixtamalization is from the Nahuatl root words, *nextli* (ashes) and *tamallii* (*tamal*). The process changes the chemical structure of the kernel, making niacin available in digestion and boosting the availability of protein. It also removes the skin from the kernel and improves the taste. Actually, the result is wonderfully nutty, aromatic, and crunchy hominy.

If you don't have the time for nixtamalization, you can certainly skip steps 1–4 and use canned hominy (*maíz pozolero*); many cooks do.

Ingredients

For the Corn

1-1/2 pounds dried white corn for pozole (*cacahuazintle*)

1 tablespoon slaked lime (calcium hydroxide; we call it "*cal*")
5 garlic cloves
1 tablespoon salt

For the Pork
2 pounds boneless pork shoulder
1-1/2 gallons water
5 garlic cloves
1 white onion, peeled and cut into quarters

For the Chile Paste
3 guajillo chiles, deseeded and deveined
2 ancho chiles
3 garlic cloves
1 tablespoon dry Mexican oregano
1 teaspoon cumin seeds

For Accompaniments
1/2 cabbage, sliced into thin strips
1 bunch radishes, thinly sliced
Mexican lime wedges

Method

For the Corn

1. The night before, place the dry corn in a large pot and fill with water 4 inches above the corn. Soak overnight.

2. The following day, discard the water and then add clean water and 1 tablespoon calcium hydroxide (cal). Bring the water to a boil and boil the corn for 15 minutes. Check doneness by taking out one kernel and rubbing between your thumb and forefinger. If the outer, slippery skin rubs off easily, the

White corn is briefly boiled with *cal* (slaked lime). The process transforms the protein structure of the corn and also removes the hull. The result is *maíz pozolero* (hominy).

1 teaspoon baking powder

1/2 teaspoon salt

4 ounces (5 fluid ounces in a cup) palm oil shortening or other nonhydrogenated vegetable shortening

1 cup water

1 teaspoon anise seeds

1 2-inch stick Mexican canela (cinnamon)

For the Egg Wash

1 egg

1 teaspoon milk

Method

For the Filling

1. Cover the pork with water. Add onion, garlic, whole cloves, and cinnamon stick, and boil, uncovered, for 1 hour or until fully cooked. Skim and discard the foam that forms on the surface.

2. Remove the pork from the broth, reserving the broth, place it on a cutting board, and chop it finely. It should look shredded.

3. Heat the oil in a skillet and sauté the pork until it becomes golden and crispy on the fibrous ends. My mom called this quality of the meat "seca."

4. Add the powdered cloves, powdered cinnamon, sugar, and salt, and mix well. Add the pecans, raisins, and 1 cup of the pork broth. Simmer on medium, scraping the bottom of the skillet to remove browned bits. When most of the liquid has evaporated, turn off the heat and set aside.

For the Dough

Preheat the oven to 350°F.

5. In a small saucepan, bring 1 cup of water to a boil. Add the cinnamon stick and anise seeds, boil for 1 minute, turn off the heat, and let it steep for 10 minutes. Drain through a sieve and set aside.

6. In a food processor, pulse all the dry ingredients for 2–3 seconds to combine them well. Add the palm oil shortening and pulse for a total of about 15 seconds until the mixture forms small granules.

7. Turn the processor back on and start pouring in the anise and cinnamon water, about 2 tablespoons at a time (you will not use all of it) until the mixture forms an elastic dough.

8. Roll it out on a floured surface with a floured rolling pin, to a 1/8-inch thickness. Use a cutter or large cup to cut out 4–5-inch diameter rounds. The extra dough will be used to make a second batch. Using a water bowl and your finger, trace a 1/4-inch stripe all around the edge of each round.

9. On half of each round, spread 2 tablespoons of filling. Fold the other half on top of the filling, making a half-moon, and press the edges to seal. The water stripe will help hold the seal.

10. Using a spatula, lift the *turcos* and place them on a greased baking sheet.

11. In a bowl, whisk together the egg and milk and brush the tops and sides of the turcos. Bake for 30–45 minutes or until they are golden brown.

Turcos are made with spiced, sweetened pork and anise-infused pastry dough.

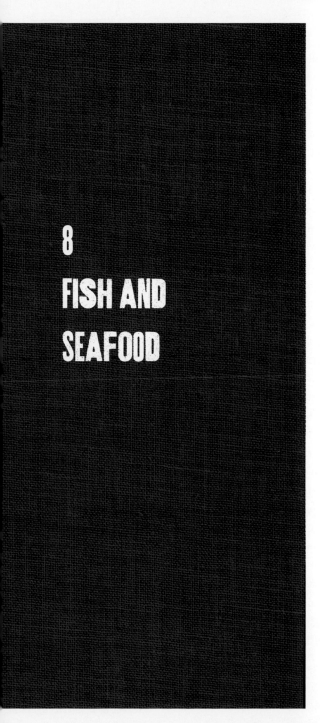

8

FISH AND SEAFOOD

Tortas de Camarón Molido | Powdered Shrimp Cakes
Recipe (makes 6 cakes)

One of the results of the Catholic religion being dominant in the indigenous Texas communities (Texas State Historical Association, 1988) is the emphasis placed on eating seafood during the 40 days of Lent. (There are actually 46 days during Lent, but Sundays are not liturgically counted.)

Perhaps creative cooks invented this smart shrimp dish to liven up the meatless days. My *amá* certainly served these little cakes regularly during Lent. The powdered shrimp does not require refrigeration so a bag of it is easy to store. The flavor is quite present, so you will enjoy that the little cakes soak up the tomato sauce and make you forget that you are doing penance.

Ingredients
1-1/2 ounces dried shrimp powder (1/2 cup)
2 eggs, separated
1/2 cup bread crumbs
Canola oil for frying
6 fresh or canned tomatoes, diced (1-1/2 cups)
1/4 teaspoon fresh minced garlic

1 teaspoon fresh or 1/4 teaspoon dry Mexican oregano

Method

1. In a blender, purée the tomatoes with the garlic and oregano. Pour the purée into a saucepan, bring it to a boil, and then lower the heat and simmer, covered, for 20–30 minutes. Hold warm.
2. In a bowl, beat the egg yolks and then add the shrimp powder and bread crumbs and mix well. Set aside.
3. In a separate bowl, whip the egg whites until they form stiff peaks. Add the shrimp mixture and combine well. The consistency should be that of a thick batter. Add a tablespoon of water if the mixture is too thick.
4. In a skillet, add canola oil to a depth of barely 1/8 inch and heat on medium until it shimmers slightly. Spoon the batter into the oil to make 4-inch cakes. Fry them about 2 minutes on each side until they are golden and crispy. Place them on paper towels.

Serve two tortas de *camarón* on each plate and top with a generous ribbon of the tomato sauce. I suggest that you serve them with *nopalitos guisados con cebolla* (page 143).

Coctel de Jaiba con Aguacate | Crab and Avocado Cocktail

Recipe (serves 4 as an appetizer)

When I bite into succulent, sweet Texas Gulf crabmeat, I am taken far back in time. It is 1528 when Karankawas find bedraggled Spaniards shipwrecked on their shores, now called Galveston Island. Lucky for the Spaniards that the Karankawa nursed and fed them.

Most anthropologists believe that the lean, dark, and tall Karankawas lived on the Texas coast for thousands of years (La Vere, 2004). We know about their food and cooking techniques from European documents, but we've lost much detail because the oral culture and traditions are lost. I can imagine Karankawa families enjoying crab cooked in different ways, much as they did corn cakes, perhaps roasting them, and seasoned with the surrounding herbs. Tragically, their life and culture reached a bloody end.

Between 1824 and 1827, Rangers under John H. Moore and Robert Kuykendall attacked them, killed most of them, and drove the survivors south. The history of this period is still being written and needs more study. We know that the surviving Karankawas fled their ancestral homeland while Kuykendall is quoted as proclaiming that "Indian hunting" had become a "sport" (Anderson, 2005).

When I'm in my kitchen cooking any type of seafood from our Texas coast, these important memories are with me. I think they make my food more substantial, nuanced, and I'm inspired to make it flavorful and appealing to all. It was the French food philosopher, Jean Anthelme Brillat-Savarin, who wrote in 1825, "Gastronomy is the intelligent knowledge of whatever concerns man's nourishment . . . the action of foods on man's morale, on his imagination, his spirit, his judgment, his courage and perceptions" (Brillat-Savarin, 2009, p. 61).

The whole point of hospitality toward friends or

Coctel de daiba con aguacate.

strangers is to enjoy. This crab cocktail that I created has three layers, each distinctive in flavor and texture, and all blend together beautifully. Oh, and yes, the dish makes me happy and helps create a table where all are welcome.

Ingredients

1/2 pound lump crabmeat, picked over, rinsed thoroughly in iced water and patted dry
4 sprigs cilantro for garnish
4 Mexican limes, sliced in half

For the Pico de Gallo

4 Roma tomatoes, diced
3 tablespoons white onion, small dice
2 tablespoons jalapeño chile, seeded, deveined, and diced small
3 tablespoons cilantro, coarsely chopped
Juice of 2 Mexican limes
1/4 teaspoon salt

For the Guacamole

2 Haas avocados, diced
1/2 tablespoon green serrano chile, sliced
1/2 tablespoon fresh cilantro, finely chopped
1 teaspoon white onion, small dice
1 teaspoon salt
1/4 cup tomato, small dice
2 tablespoons white onion, small dice
2 tablespoons fresh cilantro, coarsely chopped

Method

For the Pico de Gallo

1. Simply place all of the ingredients in a bowl and combine well.

For the Guacamole

2. Using a *molcajete*, make a fine paste of the chile, 1 teaspoon onion, 1/2 tablespoon cilantro, and salt.
3. Dice the avocado and add to the *molcajete*, scraping and folding to ensure that the avocado is covered with the seasonings.
4. Add the remaining tomato, cilantro, and onion.

To Assemble

5. In chilled sherbet glasses layer the guacamole on the bottom, then the pico de gallo (note: save some for garnish on top), and finally the lump crabmeat.
Garnish with a little pico de gallo and a sprig of cilantro. Serve with halved Mexican limes.

Cornbreaded Fried Fish

Recipe (serves 6)

This fried fish method is straightforward and reflects the penchant for coupling the flavors of fish with corn, that elemental grain that was everywhere, even in our creation stories, all the way down to what is today southern Mexico.

Even though fried fish is part of our Texas Mexican cuisine, we all know that the "fish fry" is a strong tradition throughout the U.S. South. This has developed for very good reasons: it goes back hundreds of years and it's delicious.

Ingredients

- 6 fillets, 6–8 ounces, of very fresh catfish, grouper, or cod
- 1 cup all-purpose wheat flour
- 3 eggs, well beaten
- 1 tablespoon water
- 3 cups cornmeal
- Salt to taste
- Peanut oil for deep frying

Method

1. Dry the fillets and season with salt.
2. Prepare the following: the flour on a large plate, the beaten eggs in a large bowl, and the cornmeal in a large platter or casserole.
3. Coat each fillet with the wheat flour, shaking off the excess, dip it into the eggs to coat, and then place each fillet in the cornmeal to generously coat all sides. You can hold the fillets, tucked in the cornmeal, for up to 1 hour in the refrigerator.
4. In a deep fryer or deep skillet, bring the frying oil to a temperature of 350°F and fry the fillets, taking care not to crowd the fryer. When they are a deep, dark golden color, remove with a slotted spoon and place on paper towels.

Serve immediately. I suggest that you serve it with a green vegetable, maybe *ejote con achiote* (page 137), and lemon slices.

Gorditas de Nopalitos con Camarón | Cactus and Shrimp Gorditas

Recipe (makes 25 small gorditas and 50 halves)

Ingredients

- 1 cup fresh shrimp, heads off, peeled, deveined, and cut into 1/2-inch pieces
- 1/4 cup fresh *nopales* (cactus paddles), 1/4-inch squares (To remove spines from the cactus, cover your working surface with newspaper. Use tongs to hold the cactus paddle with one hand and peel the spines off with the other hand using a potato peeler. Keep the debris and spines away from any gusts of air, as some spines are so fine that they become airborne. When finished, roll up the newspaper carefully and discard.)
- 1/4 cup white onion, small dice
- 1/8 teaspoon salt or to taste
- 1/4 cup water
- 1 tablespoon canola oil
- 1/2 cup cilantro, cut very fine
- 1/4 pound *queso fresco*

For the Gorditas
- 1 pound corn flour
- 2-1/2 cups water
- 2 teaspoons salt
- 3/4 cup canola oil

For the Chile Paste
- 1 garlic clove
- 3 ancho chiles, cleaned, seeded, and deveined
- 3 guajillo chiles, cleaned, seeded, and deveined

125

Fish and Seafood

1/2 teaspoon ground cumin

3/4 cup water

1 tablespoon canola oil

1 teaspoon salt or to taste

Method

For the Gorditas

1. Combine the corn flour, salt, oil, and water in a bowl to make a soft, moist *masa*. It should be easily pliable. Add more water if needed. Cover with a damp cloth and let stand for 20 minutes.
2. Form the dough into 25 small balls, and then flatten them to half-inch thickness.
3. Place the gorditas on 375°F griddle or *comal*. After 2 minutes flip them and cook the other side also for 2 minutes. Now that both sides are nice and crunchy, just let each side cook for another 2–3 minutes until the gorditas are golden.

For the Chile Paste (same as for tamales)

4. To devein the chiles, first lay the chile flat on a cutting board and, using a paring knife, cut a slit lengthwise. Grab the chile with one hand and with the other remove the stem along with the bunch of seeds still attached to it. Open the chile along the slit and remove the remaining seeds and veins.
5. In a large saucepan, cover the cleaned chiles with water and bring to a boil. Turn off the heat and let the chiles steep for 15 minutes so that they rehydrate and become tender.
6. Drain the chiles, discarding the water. Let the chiles cool a bit, and then place the chiles in a blender along with the garlic, cumin, and salt. Blend to a very fine paste, adding 1/2–1 cup water as needed.

For the Shrimp and Nopalitos

7. Heat the oil in a skillet on medium heat, and cook the cactus squares for 13–15 minutes. Add the onion and cook 2 minutes, stirring. Add 1/3 cup chile paste, 1/4 cup water, and combine well. Cover and cook on low for 5 minutes.
8. Add the shrimp, combine well, cover, and cook for 3 minutes, and then turn off the heat. They are ready to be served.

To Assemble

9. Using a sharp knife and a cutting board, slice each gordita along the middle, making two separate disks and lay each disk flat on a serving tray, golden side down.
10. Place 1/2 tablespoon of the shrimp mixture on each disk, and then top with a light sprinkle of queso fresco. Finish by adding just a bit of color and aroma with the freshly cut cilantro leaves.

Almejas con Tequila | Grilled Clams in Tequila Broth

Recipe (serves 4 as an appetizer)

This recipe uses ingredients that were being employed and enjoyed by our Texas Indian ancestors. Archaeologists have been able to determine that prior to 1400 clams along the coastal bays were harvested most heavily from mid April to late July. They were sometimes steamed in earth ovens lined with shells, but they were also cooked and smoked over hot rocks (Kidder, 2009).

This is another of my new recipes that I think is in keeping with the spirit of our traditional cuisine. I grill

Almejas con tequila.

the clams over an open pecan-wood fire. Then I toss them in a broth that combines tequila with the juice of tomatoes and onions. Mexican oregano finishes the dish with an aromatic flair. Grilled, smoked *elotes* (corn) make an excellent accompaniment.

Ingredients

12 clams, washed and scrubbed

2 fluid ounces good-quality white tequila.

2 Roma tomatoes, small dice

1-1/2 tablespoons white onion, minced

1 tablespoon Mexican oregano, minced

1/4 teaspoon salt

Method

1. Light a small fire using pecan wood. I use small pieces or logs of wood (10 inches) to control the heat. To ignite them, use little balls of paper towels soaked in vegetable oil if you don't have kindling. When coals form, distribute them such that you have a hot zone (you can hold your hand over the coals no more than 3 seconds) and a less hot zone (5 seconds). Alternately, use store-bought charcoal or your gas or electric grill. If you do this, I suggest adding some pecan wood chips soaked in water if you can. The smoke really imparts a wonderful taste.

2. Place the tequila, tomatoes, onion, oregano, and salt in a saucepan. Place it over the low heat zone until the onions and tomatoes get soft and a juicy broth forms. Meanwhile, relax and take a sip of tequila.

3. Place the scrubbed clams directly on the grill's hot zone. In about 5 minutes the clams will start to pop open and as they do they will absorb the pecan smoke flavor.

4. Using a spatula or a large spoon, remove the clams from the smoke, trying not to spill the juices, and place them in the tequila broth, tossing them slightly to combine all the ingredients. The shells will be very hot and help to cook the vegetables further in the clam juice.

5. At this point you can hold them warm on the grill until you are ready to serve with a nice crusty bread.

Huachinango Veracruzano | Red Snapper Veracruz Style
Recipe (serves 8)

I include this dish from Veracruz because red snapper is a delicious fish from the Gulf Coast that we share with our Veracruzan neighbors. The recipe is so delicious and colorful that it has become popular in the Texas Mexican region. Note that there is no cilantro but rather parsley. This, with olives, black pepper, and briny capers, is similar to the Moroccan Tagine dishes and is another example of Arab influence on Texas Mexican cuisine.

Because this dish makes a beautiful presentation, it is ideal for your next dinner party.

Ingredients

8 red snapper fillets, 6–8 ounces

1/4 cup juice of Mexican limes

1/4 cup extra-virgin olive oil

4 cups diced white onion

4 garlic cloves, minced

Huachinango veracruzano.

1/8 teaspoon *chile de arbol*, powdered (You can pulverize it in a *molcajete* or other mortar and pestle.)
1-1/2 teaspoons Mexican lime juice
1/8 teaspoon salt

For the Cooked Tomatillo Salsa
4 ounces fresh tomatillos (This is either a single very large one or several little ones. Total volume is 1 cup.)
1 serrano chile
1 garlic clove, unpeeled
1/8 teaspoon salt

Method
1. In a bowl, toss and coat the cabbage with the vinegars and salt. Set aside.
2. In a bowl mix together the ingredients for the Mexican lime cream and hold in the refrigerator.
3. In a saucepan, place the tomatillo, chile, and garlic. Cover with water and boil until the chile and tomatillos are fully cooked but not falling apart. They will discolor.
4. Drain them. Peel the garlic. Mash the garlic and chile in a *molcajete* until they form a paste. Add the cooked tomatillo, salt, and mash again to combine. You can do this in a blender too. Set aside in a bowl.
5. Wash the fish fillets. Dry and cut them into 3-inch × 1-inch strips. Sprinkle with salt and set aside in the refrigerator while you make the tortillas.
6. Prepare the tortillas, either fresh or store-bought, and keep them warm and moist in a container lined with cloth.
7. In a 12-inch skillet heat the peanut oil to the point

that it shimmers but before it starts to smoke. Add the pieces of fish and fry on high heat for about one minute on each side until they are opaque and fully cooked. Remove and place on paper towels.

To Assemble the Tacos
8. Divide the fish among the 6 tortillas and top with the cabbage, a spoonful of the cream sauce and then a nice spoonful of the tart tomatillo salsa.

¡Ay, dios mío!

Tortitas de Jaiba con Mayonesa de Chipotle y Yerbaniz | Crab Cakes with Chipotle-Yerbaniz Mayonnaise
Recipe (serves 8)

Oral culture and tradition regarding pre-European cooking customs along the Texas coast have been mostly lost. Thankfully archaeological evidence gives us some understanding of techniques employed in preparing seafood such as steaming in shell-lined ovens, drying, and smoking. I can imagine Karankawa families enjoying crab patties cooked in much the same way as they did corn cakes, perhaps roasting them, seasoned with herbs gathered nearby.

These Gulf Coast crab cakes are lightly flavored with onions and *chile de arbol*. The chipotle mayonnaise springs alive with the anise of the Mexican yellow-flowered aromatic herb *yerbaniz*, sometimes called Mexican tarragon.

Tortitas de jaiba con mayonesa de chipotle y yerbaniz.

Ingredients

10 ounces fresh, large, lump crabmeat

1/4 cup white onion, minced

2 tablespoons fresh flat-leaf parsley, minced

1 tablespoon fresh chives, minced

1 tablespoon fresh chives, cut into 1/2-inch pieces for garnish

1/8 teaspoon powdered chile de arbol (a.k.a. *chile arbol*)

2 egg whites

Salt to taste

Black pepper to taste

2/3 cup panko bread crumbs

3 tablespoons canola oil

For Chipotle-Yerbaniz Mayonnaise (makes 1 cup)

1 cup mayonnaise

3 chipotle chiles in adobo (canned)

3 teaspoons fresh yerbaniz (Mexican tarragon), minced

1/2 teaspoon white onion, minced

2 teaspoons fresh lemon juice

1 teaspoon salt or to taste

Method

To Make the Chipotle-Yerbaniz Mayonnaise

1. In a blender, add the mayonnaise, chipotle chile, yerbaniz, and salt. Blend until smooth, and then pour into a bowl and mix thoroughly with the minced onion and the lemon juice. Store in the refrigerator for 1 hour or even up to 6 hours for the flavors to develop.

To Make the Crab Cakes

2. Place the crabmeat in iced water, and wash and pick over the crabmeat gently so that it doesn't break apart. Set aside.

3. Sauté the onion in 1 tablespoon canola oil until soft. Set aside and allow to cool to room temperature.

4. In a large bowl mix together with a spatula the egg whites, parsley, chives, chile de arbol, salt, pepper, and cooled onion.

5. Fold in the crabmeat; when it is covered with the egg white mixture, gently fold in the panko bread crumbs.

6. Make 24 round cakes and set them aside.

7. In a skillet, preferably nonstick, heat 2 tablespoons canola oil on high heat.

8. Add the crab cakes in batches and sauté until golden, about 2 minutes on each side. Don't overcrowd them in the pan because this will lower the oil temperature too much. I use a rubber spatula and a fork to turn them gently. Add a little more canola oil if needed, just a little. Place the sautéed cakes on paper towels.

Serve immediately with the chipotle-yerbaniz mayonnaise.

9
ROOTS AND VEGETABLES

Caldo de Verduras | Vegetable Soup

Recipe (serves 6)

Ingredients

  2 quarts water

  1 turnip

  2 waxy potatoes, scrubbed, with peel

  1 *serrano chile* (Sometimes I wrap it in cheesecloth tied with
    a string, so that I can easily remove it later.)

  2 ears of corn

  2 carrots, peeled, cut into 1-inch pieces

  1 celery stick, cut into 1-inch pieces

  1/2 *chile dulce* (bell pepper), seeds removed, cut into 1/2-
    inch wide strips

  2 green onions, root tips removed and cut into 2-inch pieces

  1/4 teaspoon black peppercorns, crushed

  1 white onion, peeled, quartered

  1/2 teaspoon salt

  1/2 cup cilantro coarsely chopped

  2 limes, cut into wedges

Ejote con achiote.

Method

1. Bring the water to a boil, and add the salt, black pepper, and all the vegetables except the corn.
2. Bring the water back to a boil and then lower the heat and simmer for 35 minutes.
3. Remove the serrano chile (save it to make *salsa ranchera* another time) and add the corn. Simmer another 10 minutes.

Serve the caldo with lime wedges and chopped cilantro.

Ejote con Achiote | Haricots Verts in Achiote Sauce
Recipe (serves 4)

This is another of the handful of dishes that I include as evidence of the constant communication and sharing that happens between us in Texas and other regions to the south of the Rio Grande, a culinary exchange that has existed for thousands of years. I had to include it because I love the delicious Yucatán combination of *achiote* and orange juice.

Achiote is an iconic ingredient in Yucatán and it is derived from the seed of the *annato* tree. The little achiote seeds are found inside small pods. As a powder or paste, the achiote are deeply red and delicious. You can buy achiote paste at most grocery stores.

This recipe is my adaptation of one by Chef Roberto Santibañez.

Ingredients

- 1/4 cup mild extra-virgin olive oil
- 1 cup thinly sliced red onion
- 1/4 cup thinly sliced jalapeño chiles that have been seeded and deveined
- 3 garlic cloves, finely minced
- 3 Roma tomatoes, coarsely chopped
- 1/4 cup juice of a Seville orange (This is usually a single orange.)
- 2 teaspoons achiote paste
- 1/2 teaspoon sugar
- 1 bay leaf
- 1 teaspoon dried oregano
- 1/2 tablespoon salt
- 1 pound haricots verts or green beans

Method

1. Preheat oven to 300°F.
2. In an enameled cast-iron casserole (or stainless-steel Dutch oven), heat the olive oil and add the onions and jalapeños and cook until they are soft.
3. Add the garlic and cook for 1 minute.
4. Next, add the rest of the ingredients except the haricots verts and bring to a simmer, stirring to combine the achiote paste.
5. Add the haricots verts, stir, cover, and stew in the oven for 1–2 hours, until the beans are tender.

Serve very hot, with a smile.

Ensalada de bodas.

Ensalada de Bodas | Wedding Salad
Recipe (makes 6 cups of salad)

Ensalada de bodas has the beautiful flavor and aroma of *serrano chile* (probably my favorite chile flavor) enveloping the tang of cabbage and radishes. This recipe is from Sonora and Baja California, so the presence of Asian rice vinegar makes sense. I love this salad.

Ingredients
6 cups white cabbage, very thinly sliced and thoroughly rinsed
1 bunch radishes, thinly sliced
2 large serrano chiles, thinly sliced

For the vinaigrette
1 garlic clove
4 tablespoons extra-virgin olive oil
2 tablespoons rice vinegar
1 tablespoon apple cider vinegar
1/4 teaspoon salt or to taste

Method
1. In a bowl, cover the sliced cabbage with warm salted water and let it stand for about 20 minutes or so until it begins to become translucent. Drain well. Reserve.
2. Mash the garlic into a paste (use a garlic press or mortar) and mix it with the oil, vinegars, and salt.
3. Combine the cabbage, sliced radishes, and sliced serrano chiles, and add the vinaigrette, tossing to coat thoroughly.
Serve at room temperature.

Eggplant with Salsa Ranchera
Vegetables were a big part of our diet. When they were in season, *apá* would bring home lush-looking eggplants, firm and brightly colored. Using the technique employed for *chile relleno*, *amá* would batter (*lamprear*) them, and serve them along with refried beans and various chile salsas. These slices are elegant and light with a subtle crunch.

Ingredients
1 pound eggplant
Canola oil for frying
Salsa ranchera on page 81

For the Batter
10 ounces all-purpose wheat flour (2-1/2 cups)
1/2 teaspoon baking powder
1 teaspoon salt
1 egg
16 fluid ounces water
1/2 cup all-purpose wheat flour for dredging

Method
1. In a large bowl, mix the flour, baking powder, and salt.
2. In a small bowl, beat the egg and then add it to the dry ingredients, along with the water, and whisk until the batter is completely smooth. Keep cool in the fridge until ready to use.
3. Peel the eggplants and slice them either into rounds or lengthwise, 1/4 inch thick.
4. Place 1/2 cup of flour on a large plate and thinly coat each eggplant slice with flour, shaking off any excess. Set them aside.

139

Roots and Vegetables

5. Pour 1/4 inch canola oil in a deep skillet and heat until it just begins to shimmer. Using tongs, dip each eggplant slice in the batter to coat it completely, and then place it in the frying pan. Fry until the slices are golden, 1–2 minutes, and then turn and fry the other side. Place on paper towels and serve immediately with *salsa ranchera*.

Flor de Calabaza Rellena con Queso Panela | Squash Blossoms Stuffed with Panela Cheese
Recipe (serves 4 as a first course)

Squash blossoms abound here in spring and summer, which is not surprising since the squash is native to Mexico and grows everywhere in Texas. These squash are enjoyed battered, grilled, fried, and made into soup. The Europeans fell in love with the *calabaza* and were delighted that this little squash traveled well. It became *zucchini* in Italy and *courgette* in France.

Here, in its native land, we call it *calabacita*. The scientific name of this family of squash is *Curcubita pepo*; the flower of this particular species has great flavor and can be eaten both raw and cooked. The pistil inside the blossom should be removed after you gently wash the flower. I use scissors to snip it.

In this recipe I fill the blossoms with cheese and sauté them. Panela cheese does not melt and drip away but holds its structure. You could also use mozzarella or even ricotta if you can't find a Mexican cheese like panela. The green onion gives a gentle lift to the delicate blossom.

Whip them up for parties or serve as a first course.

Ingredients
12 zucchini squash blossoms, pistils removed
3/4 cup grated Mexican panela cheese
1-1/2 tablespoon green onion, finely minced
1 teaspoon extra virgin olive oil
Salt to taste

Method
1. In a skillet heat the olive oil, add the onions, and cook on medium heat until they are translucent, about 2 minutes. Remove from the skillet and set aside.
2. In a bowl combine well the onions and cheese. Adjust the salt.
3. Fill each squash blossom with the cheese mixture. Carefully close each and set aside.
4. In the same skillet heat 1 tablespoon olive oil.
5. In batches, add the squash blossoms and lightly sauté them on two sides, using a spatula. Add more olive oil as needed.

Flor de Calabaza Rellena con Frijol y Chorizo | Squash Blossoms Stuffed with Chorizo and Beans
Recipe (serves 4 as a first course)

This recipe is a sure "wow" factor at parties. Guests swear that the rich texture comes from cream or cheese. Actually the texture derives from the beans, slowly and properly cooked.

Ingredients

12 zucchini squash blossoms, the pistil removed
    with a knife or scissors

Canola oil for sautéing

For the Filling

Frijoles con chorizo (page 44)

Method

1. After you have removed the pistil from each squash blossom, fill a pastry bag with the bean and *chorizo* mixture and pipe 1 tablespoon into each blossom. Carefully close each blossom and set aside.
2. In a skillet, preferably nonstick, heat 1 tablespoon canola oil on medium high to the point that the surface has a slight shimmer but is not smoking. Add the blossoms and sauté them 1–2 minutes on each side so that they become a little crispy.

Serve them on individual plates or on a platter. They are delicious appetizers.

Gazpacho

Recipe (makes 1 quart)

Gazpacho is served everywhere in Texas but is not one of our traditional Texas Mexican dishes. It is a European/Arab dish—in effect, an Andalucían take on our ingredients. Gazpacho is found in Andalucía in Southern Spain, which was occupied by Arabs for over 700 years. The region has a climate similar to northern Africa, so the soup must be cold to help relieve the intense heat of the region. Absolutely essential are ingredients readily available in Andalucía: olive oil, wine vinegar, cucumbers, onion, stale bread, and garlic. The principal ingredients of the soup are Mexican: tomato and chile (in this case the nonpiquant *chile dulce*, or bell pepper). Chile dulce was naturalized into Spanish gardens after Christopher Columbus took the "sweet" chile back with him.

Because gazpacho is not Texas Mexican nor from any Mexican region, out of bounds in its flavor profile are cilantro, piquant chile, and other ingredients that would normally be flagged as part of the Mexican flavor profiles.

So, why do I include a non–Texas Mexican recipe? Because I love the soup. And I am glad that our tomatoes and chile provide inspiration to others. This recipe makes a complex, soothing, and highly refreshing soup. I omit the strong onion flavor altogether. I also omit the bread, which is standard in the Spanish recipes, because I fiercely blend the ingredients. This causes emulsification of the olive oil and achieves body and creaminess. The olive oil is present in the taste, but serves as a background.

Ingredients

2 pounds tomatoes, diced (6 cups)

1/4 pound red *chile dulce* (bell pepper), diced (1 cup)

1/4 pound cucumber, peeled and diced (3/4 cup)

2 garlic cloves, peeled and crushed

2 fluid ounces red wine vinegar

4 fluid ounces extra-virgin olive oil, Spanish if at all possible

1-1/2 teaspoon kosher salt

141

Nopalitos guisados con cebolla.

Method

1. Wash all the fruits. I scrub them in a strong solution of salt water, and then rinse them.
2. Place all the ingredients in a blender and churn away until the purée is creamy. In fact, it should be so creamy that it looks almost like a cream-based soup. You may have to do this in batches.
3. Chill in the fridge for 4 hours or an entire day so that the flavors blend.
4. It's ready, and very simple to make. Stir vigorously before serving and garnish with croutons and small cucumber dice.

Nopalitos Guisados con Cebolla | Cactus Sautéed with Onion

Recipe (serves 6)

Ingredients

6 fresh *nopales* (cactus paddles), cleaned of all spines, rinsed, and cut into 1/2-inch squares
1 white onion, thinly sliced
2 tablespoons canola or other vegetable oil
1/4 teaspoon salt

Method

1. To remove spines from the cactus, cover your working surface with newspaper. Use tongs to hold the cactus paddle with one hand and peel the spines off with the other hand using a potato peeler. Keep the debris and spines away from any gusts of air, as some spines are so fine that they become airborne. When finished, roll up the newspaper carefully and discard.
2. Heat the canola oil on medium heat and sauté the *nopales* for 13 minutes. They will acquire some golden color and most of the liquid will evaporate.
3. Add the sliced onions and salt, and cook until the white onion is soft and translucent but not brown. Adjust the salt and serve immediately.

Pepino y Jícama con Chile y Limón | Cucumbers and Jícama with Serrano Chile Dressing

Recipe (serves 4)

We ate lots of vegetables, many of them raw, and what we ate depended on the season. We enjoyed a bite or bites at all times throughout the day. *Amá* would slice them onto a plate and put it on the kitchen table: radishes, cucumber, jícama, turnips, carrots, and so on. Limes, salt, and chiles were placed alongside.

Of course, anytime we went by the kitchen, we'd squeeze lime on them, maybe some chile, and create a refreshing, sparky combination. This is a new recipe that I created, inspired by amá's plate of fresh, crispy vegetables, citrus, and chiles. For a twist, I add a touch of *yerbaniz* or *pericón*, an aromatic herb native to Mexico and common here in Texas. My niece Christine brushed past it in my garden the other day and was startled by the aroma. "Oh, my God, I have not smelled that since I was a child with grandmother Florencia!" The leaves from the yerbaniz make a restorative tea for colds and stomach aches and Christine's paternal grandmother used to make it for her whenever she was sick. My niece, delighted and surprised, had not smelled nor tasted it since childhood.

143

Sometimes called anise blossom or Mexican tarragon, be sure to use just a touch, as indicated in the recipe. If you use more, it will completely overpower all the other flavors, which is not desirable. I have noted in the recipe that it is optional. If you are unable to find the herb, the salad will still be wonderfully bright and refreshing.

Ingredients

1 cup cucumber, peeled, seeds removed, and cut into 1/4-inch by 1-inch sticks

1 cup jícama, peeled and cut into 1/4-inch cubes

1/2 cup radishes, each radish cut into six very small wedges

1/2 teaspoon serrano chile, minced

2 tablespoons extra-virgin olive oil

1/4 teaspoon salt

1/8 teaspoon yerbaniz a.k.a. Mexican tarragon (optional)

2 tablespoons fresh lime juice

Method

1. In a *molcajete*, make a smooth paste with the serrano chile and salt, and then add the olive oil and blend together. Add the lime juice and whisk to emulsify. Set aside.

2. Place all sticks, cubes, and wedges in a bowl, add the molcajete dressing, and combine. Chill for 30 minutes, and then fold in barely 1/8 teaspoon finely minced yerbaniz.

Serve as a snack or to accompany lunch or dinner dishes.

Pepino y jícama con chile y limón.

10

RICE AND PASTA

Arroz con Almendras | Rice with Almonds

Recipe (serves 4)

Ingredients

1 cup white rice
2 tablespoons canola or other vegetable oil
2 tablespoons white onion, minced
2 tablespoons celery, minced
5 tablespoons slivered almonds
1 garlic clove, minced
2 cups water
1/8 teaspoon salt

Method

1. Heat the oil in a saucepan over medium heat. Add the onion and celery and cook until translucent, about 1–2 minutes. Add the minced garlic and cook another minute.
2. Add the rice, slivered almonds, and water, and bring to a boil. Turn down the heat and cook at a very slow simmer, covered, for 15 minutes.

Arroz con Cilantro | Rice with Cilantro

Recipe (serves 4)

The color of this dish is bright and the cilantro aroma is sumptuous. I sometimes eat it just by itself.

Ingredients

- 1 cup rice
- 1 tablespoon canola or other vegetable oil
- 1 teaspoon salt
- 2 tablespoons green onion, finely sliced
- 1 cup packed cilantro, minced, divided into 2 half-cup portions
- 2 cups water

Method

1. Heat the oil in a saucepan, add the rice, and cook for 2 minutes. Add the green onion and cook for 1 minute.
2. Add the water, salt, and 1/2 cup of the cilantro. Bring the water to a boil, and then lower the heat to a low simmer, cover and cook for 12–15 minutes.
3. When the rice is cooked, add the other 1/2 cup of cilantro and gently toss with a large fork or tine. It is ready to serve.

Texas Mexican Rice

Recipe (serves 4)

This rice is fluffy and delicate. It has a full nutty taste with just a bit of color from tomatoes, a slight undercurrent of cumin, and, most importantly, no heavy lard to hide the rice flavor.

Ingredients

- 1 cup long grain rice
- 1 tablespoon canola oil (optional)
- 2 cups water
- 1/2 teaspoon cumin
- 1/4 teaspoon black peppercorns
- 1/2 teaspoon salt
- 1 garlic clove
- 1 small tomato, diced and crushed

Method

1. In a *molcajete* make a paste of the cumin, black peppercorns, salt, and garlic.
2. In a deep skillet add the oil and cook the rice over medium heat until it begins to take on some color, about 3 minutes.
3. Add a little water to the molcajete to scrape the paste from the sides and pour it into the rice, being careful with the splatter. Add the rest of the water and the crushed tomato and its juice, and stir the ingredients to mix well.
4. Reduce heat to low, cover tightly, and cook for 15 minutes.

Adjust the salt. The rice will be tender, fluffy, and gently aromatic of cumin and black pepper.

Fideo | Coil Vermicelli

Recipe (serves 4)

Fideo is another of our classic dishes, and yet it is so very recent, the addition of pasta into our cuisine. I grew up with this flavorful coiled vermicelli stewed with tomatoes, onions, and garlic. Sometimes the pasta would be shell-shaped, the Italian *conchieglie*. We call them *conchitas*. In our house, the eggs were optional, but some families include the eggs religiously.

I often wonder what the Italians would have done without our tomatoes. Here's what we do with their pasta. Thank the heavens for friendly cultural encounters.

Ingredients

2 Roma tomatoes, diced (or 4 ounces canned tomato sauce)
1 small white onion, sliced
1 clove garlic
8 black peppercorns
1/2 teaspoon salt
1/8 teaspoon, or slightly less, cumin
1/2 pound fideo (coiled vermicelli)
5 cups water
2 tablespoons canola or other vegetable oil
4 eggs, hard-boiled

Method

1. In a *molcajete* mash the black pepper, garlic, salt, and cumin into a fine paste. Set aside.
2. In a large sauté pan, heat the oil and sauté the vermicelli until it acquires some golden color, about 2 minutes. Add the onion and continue cooking until the onion is translucent.
3. Add a little water to the molcajete to scrape the paste from the sides and add it to the vermicelli. Add the tomatoes or tomato sauce and the rest of the water. Bring to a boil and cook for 12 minutes until the pasta is cooked and the liquid is reduced. Adjust the salt.
4. Slice the hard-boiled eggs and place them atop the fideo.

Serve immediately.

147

Agua de Jamaica.

11

BEVERAGES

Agua de Jamaica | Hibiscus Drink

Recipe (makes 2 quarts)

Agua de Jamaica is as colorful as it is refreshing. I love the delicious tart taste.

It is enjoyed here, as well as all over Mexico and Central America. Hibiscus flowers are boiled in water with a little sugar, that's all. I suggest you make and taste this exactly as described in the recipe so that you can experience how it is enjoyed in this region. It seems to me richer and more peace-like to understand a people and their taste first, before changing their food.

Ingredients
  2 quarts filtered water
  3/4 cup dried flores de Jamaica (hibiscus flowers)
  1/2 cup sugar or 1/3 cup light agave nectar

Method
1. Bring the water to a boil, add the flowers, and boil for 15 minutes
2. Turn off the heat and let the water cool to room temperature

3. Strain through a fine-mesh sieve, add the sugar or agave nectar, and cool in the fridge for 2 hours. Serve over ice.

Ahem, I add 2 ounces of vodka to my glass of agua de Jamaica and I call it the Karankawa. A nice switch from the Cape Cod cocktail.

Agua de Pepino con Limón | Cucumber and Lime Drink

Recipe (makes 2 quarts)

Pair lime with cucumber and, yes, you can take a miraculous, blessed break from the Texas heat. Picking cotton or hoeing sugar beets is no picnic. During short breaks we would sit under the shade of the truck, break open a cucumber, and bite into it. I was ever so grateful for this juicy and refreshing moment before having to go back into the sun.

Asia and India are where the *pepino* first grew and, *gracias a dios*, it made its way here where we now consider it our own. This *agua fresca* recipe has hardly any sugar. The small amount of fresh lime serves to perk up the cucumber flavor, so you really should not taste lime as a separate flavor. This because we are not making cucumber limeade. Agua means water. If you keep this in mind you will steer clear of making cucumber juice or cucumber-flavored limeade. All aguas frescas are naturally flavored ice-cold water.

Ingredients
- 2 cucumbers, about 8 inches long, peeled, chopped coarsely
- 2 quarts filtered water

2-1/2 tablespoons sugar
1 small lime, skin and white pith removed

Method
1. Place all the ingredients in the blender and blend on high.
2. Keep it going until there are no small particles and the beverage is completely smooth. If there are some particles in it and you are a stickler like me, strain it through a fine-mesh sieve.

Chill it for a couple of hours and serve with lots of ice.

Agua de Tamarindo | Tamarind Drink

Recipe (makes 2 quarts)

If you've not had occasion to try this, I really urge you to take a sip. It's somewhat tart but you'll find it is also wonderfully complex, not at all like a sugary one-dimensional soft drink. It is a standard *agua fresca*, popular all over Texas and Mexico, and is yet another example of how food pathways impact civilization and culture. Tamarind is African, found in the tropical areas of the continent from where it migrated to Arabia. It arrived in our region in the 1500s with the Spaniards whose food and culture had already been influenced by the Arabs who occupied Spain for hundreds of years. It has become an integral part of our culture now and we use it not just for beverages but also for candies and pastries.

Do try this recipe and keep a full pitcher in your fridge. Oh, it has diuretic properties when consumed in large enough quantities.

Tamarind, peeled.

Agua de tamarindo.

3. Pour the mixture into a pitcher and add sugar according to your taste. Chill thoroughly, at least 2 hours.

Serve over ice.

Margarita
Recipe (makes 1 cocktail)

I love this cocktail because it has fresh lime juice, does not hide the tequila taste, and is not too sweet. I use the Mexican Controy because of its straightforward orange taste. My great hope is that one day every restaurant that serves margaritas will use fresh lime juice and good tequila.

Ingredients
3 ounces tequila, white
1 ounce Mexican Controy (If you can't get Controy, use triple sec. I do not like the French Cointreau because I find it too unctuous for a tart margarita.)
1 ounce fresh Mexican lime juice
Ice
Coarse salt for the glass

Method
1. Coat the rim of a coupe glass with the juice of a lime and dip it in a plate of coarse salt to line the glass. Set aside.
2. In a cocktail shaker, add all the margarita ingredients and shake vigorously. Strain and pour into the salted coupe glass. Tiny ice crystals will float on the surface, inviting you to sip.

Red Jalapeño Champagne Cocktail
Recipe (makes 4 drinks)

This recipe steers away from traditional Texas Mexican flavors. But I like it, so here it is. I created this cocktail for the Latin American Chamber of Commerce of Georgia. They asked me to design a signature cocktail for a special event honoring Southwest Airlines as they initiated new routes into the Atlanta market. I readily took on the challenge to achieve what they wanted: an elegant cocktail that would be representative of their Latino membership and of Georgia, and, alas, nonalcoholic.

I named it the Southwest Sunrise, and it was the perfect toast at the elegant event.

For the current recipe, I went ahead and added sparkling wine so that it is truly a red jalapeño champagne cocktail, and now I call it the Southwest Sunrise Royale! I think the pectin in the red jalapeño jelly gives the drink a sensuous mouth feel.

Ingredients
4 fluid ounces peach nectar, chilled
4 fluid ounces guava juice, chilled
2 fluid ounces tamarind juice, chilled
2 teaspoons red jalapeño jelly
4 teaspoons Mexican lime juice, chilled
8 fluid ounces champagne or sparkling wine, chilled
Thin slices of lime peel for garnish and aroma

Red jalapeño champagne cocktail.

Method

1. Blend all the ingredients except the sparkling wine and lime peels in a blender until the jalapeño jelly is completely blended and a froth has developed.
2. Add the sparkling wine and then pour into four white wine glasses and garnish with lime peel.

Sangría

Recipe (serves 4)

Although sangría is totally Spanish, we drink it everywhere around here. I am proud of how many weddings and birthday parties my recipe has enlivened. I learned the recipe during one of my stays in Toledo. No, not Ohio.

I've made the recipe precise so that it's easy to follow, and you can be sure that it will be delicious every time. But most often sangría will be thrown together with available fresh fruit, the only rule being to respect its heritage and confluence of flavors.

Ingredients

1 cup unpeeled diced ripe peach (usually 1 peach)

1/2 cup peeled, diced Seville orange (usually 1 small orange)

1 tablespoon sugar (You can increase this by 1/2 tablespoon or 1 tablespoon if the fruits are not very sweet.)

1 tablespoon freshly squeezed lemon juice

1/4 cup freshly squeezed Seville orange juice (usually 1 small orange)

1 2-inch cinnamon stick (Wrap the cinnamon in cheesecloth so that there are no splinters in the drink.)

3/4 cup brandy

1 bottle red wine (I like either a cabernet sauvignon from Argentina or Chile or a rioja from Spain.)

6 ounces lemon-lime soda (optional but recommended)

Method

1. In a pitcher place the diced peach, diced orange, brandy, and sugar. Smash the fruit a little with a wooden spoon and let stand for 15 minutes.
2. Add the orange juice, lemon juice, wine, and cinnamon, and place in the refrigerator for 1–2 hours until very well chilled.
3. Just before serving, remove the cinnamon and add 6 ounces lemon-lime soda. Stir gently.

I like to serve the sangría in double old-fashioned glasses with a few ice cubes.

12
SWEETS

Arroz con Leche | Rice with Milk

Recipe (serves 4)

There are certain recipes that remind you of your mother and father and brothers and sisters and just good times at home. This is one of them. As you have seen with many of the recipes in this book, the best things in life are often really simple.

Ingredients

- 1/2 cup white rice
- 2-1/4 cups water
- 2-inch stick Mexican *canela* (cinnamon)
- 1/4 cup black raisins
- 2 tablespoons sugar
- 1 cup milk

Method

1. Bring the water, cinnamon stick, and rice to a boil, lower the heat, and simmer for 25 minutes. Then add the milk and sugar, and cook for another 5 minutes.
2. Remove the cinnamon stick, add the raisins, and stir. The raisins will plump within seconds and then it is ready to serve.

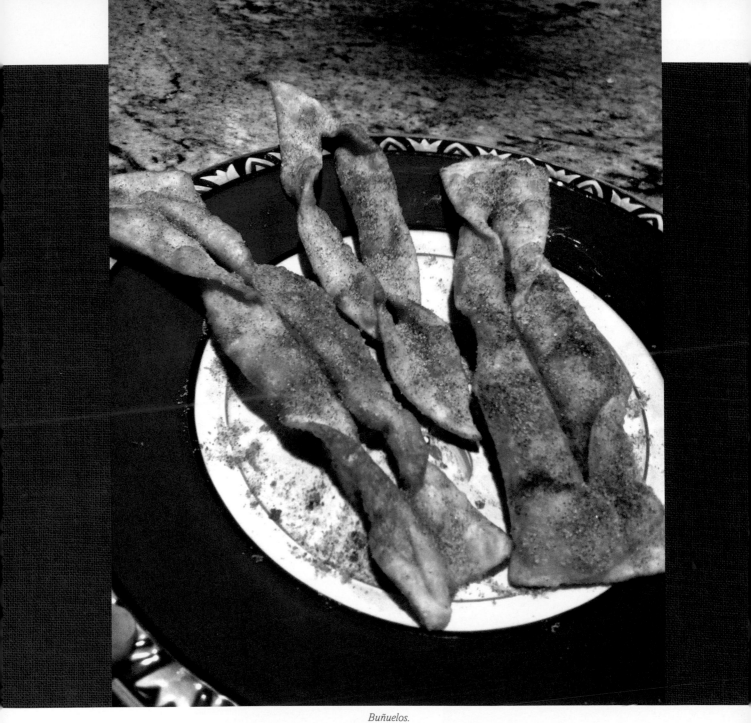

Buñuelos.

Buñuelos | Fried Cinnamon Crisps

Recipe (makes 3 dozen)

New Year's Eve meant *buñuelos* at our home. My mom shaped them like little twirling ribbons, golden and glistening with cinnamon and sugar, and we enjoyed them with hot chocolate.

Ingredients

One-half of the recipe for wheat tortillas (page 59), with the addition of 1 teaspoon sugar per cup of flour

Canola oil or peanut oil for frying

3/4 cup granulated sugar

2 tablespoons ground Mexican *canela* (cinnamon)

Method

1. Mix the sugar and ground canela in a bowl and set aside.
2. Make the wheat tortillas as on page 59, but add 1 teaspoon sugar per cup of flour.
3. After rolling a round tortilla, slice it into 2-inch wide strips. In the middle of each strip, cut a slit lengthwise with a knife, leaving 1 inch on each end uncut.
4. Take each strip and insert one end through the slit. As you do so, it will form a cheery twisting ribbon.
5. Heat the oil in a deep skillet or deep fryer to the point of shimmering at 350°F.
6. Add the tortilla ribbons, turning as needed, until both sides turn golden and crispy. This will take about 2 minutes.
7. Place on paper towels and sprinkle with generous dashes of the cinnamon and sugar mixture.

This is a great fiesta tradition. The kids will devour them and the adults will fight over them.

Capirotada | Lenten Bread Pudding

Every Holy Week my *amá*, Dominga Medrano, would gift us with *capirotada*. Our kitchen overflowed with aromas of cinnamon, cilantro, and *piloncillo*, and even now I can see her face serving us this bread pudding on Good Friday. Food is such a sacred, happy gift.

Recipe (serves 12)

Ingredients

5 cups water

1 5-inch stick Mexican *canela* (cinnamon)

1 cup black raisins

5 ounces piloncillo, scraped into small pieces (You can use brown sugar but it's worth the effort to try to find piloncillo. Piloncillo is made by crushing sugarcane, boiling the juice, and placing it into conic molds. The flavor is complex with hints of smoke and caramel.)

1 cup pecans, coarsely chopped

2 cups mild cheddar cheese, shredded

1/4 cup cilantro, coarsely chopped

12-inch loaf French bread

Method

Preheat oven to 350°F.

1. Add the canela and piloncillo to the water and bring to a boil. Turn off the heat and let steep for 20

159

Sweets

Capirotuda.

minutes, stirring as needed to dissolve all of the piloncillo.

2. Make 3 layers of the French loaf by horizontally slicing it lengthwise.
3. Arrange the bottom layer in the pan; add 1/3 of the cheese, 1/3 of the pecans, and 1/3 of the raisins, spreading everything evenly.
4. Place the second bread layer and again spread another 1/3 of the cheese, pecans, and raisins.
5. Place the topmost bread layer and then spread the remaining cheese, pecans, raisins, and the cilantro.
6. Pour the *piloncillo* and *canela* water on top of the bread loaf, using a strainer as needed to strain out any bits of cinnamon stick.
7. Cover the dish and bake for 30 minutes or until the cheese is melted and bubbling.

Empanadas de Camote | Sweet Potato Empanadas
Recipe (makes 24 4-inch empanadas)

Pastries are a French contribution to our cuisine. These make use of our native sweet potato, taking advantage of its natural sugars and creamy texture.

Ingredients
2 pounds sweet potatoes
4 tablespoons *piloncillo* or brown sugar

For the Dough
1 pound all-purpose wheat flour
1/2 cup sugar
1 teaspoon baking powder
1/2 teaspoon salt
4 ounces (5 fluid ounces in a cup) palm oil shortening or other nonhydrogenated vegetable shortening
1 teaspoon anise seeds
1 2-inch stick Mexican *canela* (cinnamon)

For the Egg Wash
1 egg
1 teaspoon milk

Method

For the Filling
1. Cover the sweet potatoes with water, bring to a boil, and cook for 25–30 minutes until they are completely cooked and soft when pierced with a fork. Drain them. Peel them and mash with a masher, food mill, or food processor until they are smooth.
2. Place them in a saucepan, add the piloncillo or brown sugar, and cook over medium heat for 5 minutes, long enough for the piloncillo to dissolve and distribute evenly. If the mixture is too dry, add 2 tablespoons of water. The desired texture is a not too moist paste. Set aside to cool until you are ready to assemble the empanadas.

For the Dough
Preheat the oven to 350°F
3. In a small saucepan bring 1 cup of water to a boil. Add the cinnamon and anise seeds, boil for 1 minute, turn off the heat, and let it steep for 10 minutes. Strain with a sieve.
4. In a food processor, pulse together all the dry in-

gredients to combine them well. Add the palm oil shortening and pulse for a total of about 15 seconds until the mixture forms small granules.

5. Turn the processor back on and immediately start pouring in the anise and cinnamon water slowly, about 2 tablespoons at a time (you will not use all of it) until the mixture forms an elastic dough.

6. Roll it out on a floured surface with a floured rolling pin, to a 1/8-inch thickness. Use a cutter or bowl to cut out 4–5-inch diameter rounds. Using a water bowl and your finger, trace a 1/4-inch stripe all around the edge of each round. The extra dough will be used to make a second batch.

7. On half of each round, spread 2 tablespoons of the sweet potato filling, fold the other half on top of the filling while making a half-moon, and press the edges firmly to seal. The water stripe will help hold the seal.

8. Using a spatula, lift the empanadas and place them on a greased baking sheet.

9. In a bowl, whisk together the egg and milk and brush the tops and sides of the empanadas. Bake for 30–45 minutes or until they are golden brown.

Hojarascas | Cinnamon Cookies
Recipe (makes 2 dozen)

These are classic Texas Mexican. My childhood is marked by these cookies that veritably crumble when you hold them. They were at every wedding and every special anniversary. But I could not find the recipe for the right proportions to get that crumble and cinnamon taste. Gracias to my oldest sister, Nieves Ortega, who rummaged through boxes in her home and eventually found her own handwritten note with the recipe. This is our gift to you. Christmas is a good time for these as well. The cinnamon is nice.

Ingredients
2 cup all-purpose wheat flour

2/3 cup sugar

1 egg

1/4 teaspoon baking powder

1 teaspoon ground cinnamon

2/3 cup palm oil shortening or other nonhydrogenated vegetable shortening

For the Sugar Coating
1 cup sugar

2 tablespoons ground cinnamon

Method
Preheat oven to 350°F.

1. In a wide-mouth bowl, mix the sugar coating ingredients and set aside.

2. In a food processor, pulse and mix all the dry ingredients well.

3. Add the palm oil shortening and egg and pulse until the ingredients form small granules, about 15 seconds.

4. Form 1/2 tablespoon-sized balls and place them 1 inch apart on a nongreased cookie sheet.

5. Lightly coat the bottom of a flat cup with sugar and press the balls down to 1/2-inch thickness.

6. Bake for 15 minutes exactly, not longer. The cookies will look deceptively white and pale. That's perfect.

Hojarascas.

Mazapán.

7. While hot and just out of the oven, coat each cookie with the sugar cinnamon mixture. They are fragile so take care not to break them. As they cool they will harden and become less fragile.

The cookies will keep easily for 1 week, but they never survive that long.

Mazapán | Peanut Candy
Recipe (makes 2 dozen candies)

A cousin of marzipan, which is made with almonds and sugar and originates in Asia and the Middle East, mazapán is distinctly Mexican in that it replaces the almonds with peanuts, which are of Latin American origin, and adds corn, which is, of course, native to Mexico. To maintain the *cacahuate* (peanut) flavor, the candy is not cooked. You will be amazed at how simple this is to make. Once you bite into these, you'll love the almost peanut-butter-sweet taste. Some of my friends have called these "Ruiz's pieces."

Ingredients
6 ounces unsalted peeled peanuts
3 ounces confectioner's sugar (contains corn starch)

Method
1. In a food processor, process the ingredients until they form a stiff dough that feels like putty.
2. Roll out the dough to a 1/4-inch thickness.
3. Using a round fluted cutter, cut little round wafers and set aside for storage.

They are ready to eat!

Watermelon Canapé with Avocado, Serrano Chile, and Grapes
Recipe (makes 24 watermelon canapés)

Summer watermelons can become formal for a dress-up party. Here I make watermelon wafers and place them on a thin jícama wafer. The filling is spicy guacamole with grapes. A sliver of fried yucca finishes the canapé with a starchy crunch. Be forewarned that this recipe is for experienced cooks who love to spend time in the kitchen. These canapés are labor intensive, a pleasure to make and share.

I created the dish for a morning television show whose producers wanted to feature watermelons in season. I prepared all the ingredients and was ready to go on camera. The TV crew never showed up. Miffed for just a second, I moved on and shared these tidbits with my friends and we had a delicious breakfast treat!

Interestingly, as I was creating this dish I thought to myself, "That's not the straightforward, unfancy, working-class cuisine of Chicanos." But I wanted to twist a bit and be inventive, and it provides an instance to argue with my chef friends about whether this dish is truly Texas Mexican.

Ingredients
1 seedless watermelon
1 jícama
1 yucca root
1/2 serrano chile, sliced
1 tablespoon white onion, diced
1 Haas avocado (*aguacate*), sliced into small cubes
3 seedless white grapes, each grape quartered

Watermelon canapé with avocado, serrano chile, and grapes.

3 seedless red grapes, each grape quartered

1/2 teaspoon salt

Method

First, assemble all of the elements.

Jícama

1. Peel the jícama and slice it into very thin wafers using a mandoline.
2. Using a 2-inch fluted cutter, cut the jícama wafers into fluted discs. Set aside and chill.

Yucca

3. Peel one yucca root and, using a mandoline, make very thin wafers.
4. Cut wafers into strips 1/4 inch wide and 2 inches long.
5. Fry the strips in a deep fryer at 360°F until golden. This will take only a few seconds.
6. Remove from the fryer, place on a wire rack, and salt evenly. Set aside.

Watermelon

7. Peel a seedless watermelon and cut into large slices 3/4 inch thick.
8. Using a 1-3/4–inch fluted cutter (smaller than the one for the jícama), make watermelon rounds.
9. In each round, scoop out some of the center, making a small hole that does not cut all the way through. This is for the filling. Set these aside and keep them chilled.

Guacamole with Grapes

10. In a *molcajete*, place 1/2 sliced serrano chile, 1 tablespoon diced white onion, and 1/2 teaspoon salt. Grind into a smooth paste.
11. Add 1 large Haas avocado, sliced into small cubes, and blend thoroughly so that the serrano chile paste coats the avocado cubes.
12. Fold in the quartered grapes. Set aside.

To Assemble the Canapés

13. Spoon the guacamole into each watermelon round, place on the jícama wafer, and top with a sliver of fried yucca.

Serve immediately and celebrate the Texas Mexican summer in style. Don't think about television crews.

Raspa de Sandía | Watermelon Ice with Blueberries

Recipe (serves 8)

For a summer dinner, I thought up this watermelon raspa with blueberries and lime, which is refreshing and visually beautiful. It is simply a snow cone, done up for grown-ups.

Ingredients

1 cup sugar and 1 cup water to make simple syrup (Combine the sugar and water and bring to a boil, making sure all the sugar is dissolved, and then cool down to room temperature.)

8 cups diced seedless watermelon without the rind

3 tablespoons freshly squeezed Mexican lime juice

About 60 fresh blueberries

8 Mexican lime wedges

Raspa de sandía y Campari.

Method

1. Place the watermelon and 2/3 cup of the simple syrup in a blender and blend until it is a completely smooth and very fine purée. There should not be any noticeable pulp. If after blending it, the watermelon purée still has noticeable pulp, strain it through a coarse-mesh sieve.
2. Add the lime juice and taste, adjusting the sweetness with additional simple syrup or lime juice as necessary. The purée should be sweet with a very slight, subtle tang from the lime.
3. Pour the watermelon purée into a 9-inch or larger baking dish and place it in the freezer. After 45 minutes, scrape the sides of the dish and push the frozen crystals to the center of the dish. Thereafter do this every 30 minutes, making sure that fine crystals form evenly with no big chunks. Total time will be about 3 hours.

Serve the iced watermelon in individual cups or bowls and top with blueberries and the lime wedge.

Raspa de Sandía y Campari | Watermelon and Campari Sorbet
Recipe (serves 4)

This refreshing dessert is another new recipe, an example of cooks constantly remaining current by carefully observing and relating to their local context. It has only three ingredients, and correct ratio/blending is the feat.

Although not native to the region, the *sandía* has become a Texas Mexican staple, as any Mexican American family will tell you. Watermelon (*sandía*) and Mexican lime are a natural blend in *agua fresca*, of course, but the addition of Italian Campari may give you pause. Fear not, for it harmonizes beautifully. How did I get this idea? By looking at our Texas cactus.

Italy's Campari was already connected to Mexico and our Texas Mexican region because when it was first invented, and until 2006, its color used to come from the crushed cochineal beetle that lives in the nopal cactus of Texas and Mexico (Burgner, 2012). The little insects are in those white powdery specks that you see on cactus paddles.

Our ancestors, the Texas Native Americans, had discovered and widely used the beautiful radiant red color (Dial and Black, 2007). Until recently Starbucks used it to produce the hue in its strawberry frappucino (Straus, 2012).

The right proportions and blending make this a truly complex bitter-tart-sweet, grown-up dessert. Glazed spearmint adds contrast both in texture and color.

Ingredients

4 cups watermelon cubes
2-1/2 tablespoons Mexican lime juice
1-1/2 fluid ounces simple syrup (Make simple syrup by combining equal parts sugar and water and heating until fully dissolved. Cool to room temperature.)
3 ounces Campari
12 spearmint leaves

For Mint Glaze
1/2 cup sugar
1/2 cup water
1 tablespoon corn syrup

169

Method

1. In a blender, blend the watermelon, lime juice, syrup, and Campari until totally smooth.

2. Pour the watermelon purée into a 9-inch or larger baking dish and place it in the freezer. After 45 minutes, scrape the sides of the dish and push the frozen crystals to the center of the dish. Thereafter do this every 30 minutes, making sure that fine crystals form evenly with no big chunks. Total time will be about 3 hours.

3. To glaze the spearmint leaves, heat the three mint glaze ingredients in a small pan. Heat gradually to the point where if you drop the syrup into a cup of cold water it forms a firm ball. The syrup temperature at this stage is 245°F. Remove from heat. After the syrup cools down, dip the mint leaves, shake off excess, and place them on a platter until you are ready to garnish. (I learned this candying technique from my mother because she was always making red candied apples on Sundays to help raise money for our Catholic parish church. The candy glaze was beautifully red, glass-like, and delicious. Keep this glaze recipe for other uses.)

When ready to serve, scoop into sorbet dishes and garnish with the glazed spearmint. The spearmint adds a wonderful finishing taste to the sorbet. In Spanish we call it *yerba buena*, the good herb.

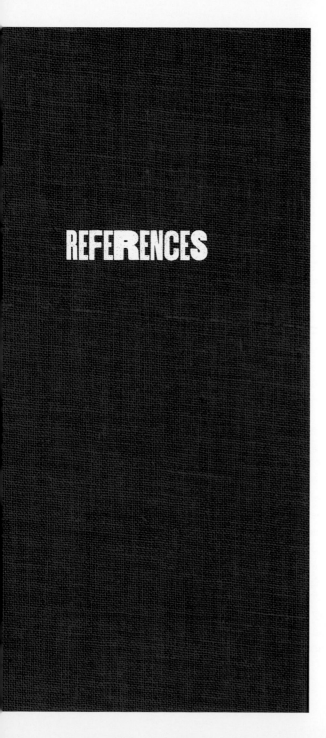

REFERENCES

Anderson, G. C. (1999). *The Indian Southwest, 1580–1830: Ethnogenesis and Reinvention.* Norman: University of Oklahoma Press.

———. (2005). *The Conquest of Texas Ethnic Cleansing in the Promised Land, 1820–1875.* Norman: University of Oklahoma Press.

Bastian, D. E., and Mitchell, J. K. (2004). *Handbook of Native American Mythology.* Santa Barbara, CA.: ABC-CLIO. Retrieved from http://books.google.com/books?id=IsyQu1kDK-kC&dq=maize native american mythology&source=gbs_navlinks_s.

Berdan, F. F., and Anawalt, P. R. (1997). *The Essential Codex Mendoza.* Berkeley and Los Angeles: University of California Press.

Berzok, L. M. (2005). *American Indian Food.* Westport, Conn.: Greenwood Press.

Black, S., and Dial, S. (2006). "Olmos Dam." Retrieved from http://www.texasbeyondhistory.net/st-plains/images/ap10.html.

Brillat-Savarin, J. A. (2009). *The Physiology of Taste.* New York: Alfred A. Knopf, Inc.

Burgner, A. (2012). "Change in Beetle-Juice Recipe Is Haunting the Purists." Retrieved from http://www.timeslive.co.za/opinion/columnists/2012/12/05/change-in-beetle-juice-recipe-is-haunting-the-purists.

Cabeza de Vaca, A. N. (2003). *The Narrative of Cabeza de Vaca.* (Adorno, R., and Pautz, P. C., eds., trans.). Lincoln: University of Nebraska Press.

Center for Food Safety. (n.d.). *GE Food.* Retrieved from http://truefoodnow.org/campaigns/genetically-engineered-foods/.

Crandall, B. (2012). *McAllen Revealed as Nation's Most Impoverished Community.* Retrieved from http://www.valleycentral.com/news/story.aspx?list=195030&id=805449.

Dial, S. (2006). "Birds." Retrieved from http://www.texasbe-yondhistory.net/st-plains/nature/images/birds.html.

———. (2012). *Texas beyond History: Texas Archaeological Research Laboratory, University of Texas at Austin.* Austin: University of Texas. Retrieved from http://www.texas-beyondhistory.net/st-plains/images/ap1.html.

Dial, S., and Black, S. (2005). "Clams and Snails." Retrieved from http://www.texasbeyondhistory.net/plateaus/na-ture/images/clams.html.

———. (2007). "Texas beyond History: Fantastic Facts." Retrieved from http://www.texasbeyondhistory.net/kids/facts-new.html.

———. (2009). "Shellfish." Retrieved from http://www.texasbeyondhistory.net/coast/nature/images/shellfish.html.

———. (2010). "Amaranth, Pigweed, Quelite." Retrieved from http://www.texasbeyondhistory.net/st-plains/na-ture/images/amaranth.html.

Dockall, J. E., and Black, S. (2007). "Morhiss Evidence." Retrieved from http://www.texasbeyondhistory.net/morhiss/index.html.

Foster, W. C. (1995). *Spanish Expeditions into Texas, 1689–1768.* Austin: University of Texas Press.

Garibay, A.M. (2006). *Historia general de las cosas de Nueva España escrita por Fr. Bernardino de Sahagún.* Mexico City: Editorial Porrúa.

Gtatschet, A. S., Hammond, C. A., and Oliver, A. W. B. (1891). *The Karankawa Indians, the Coast People of Texas.* Cambridge, Mass.: Peabody Museum of American Archaeology and Ethnology. Retrieved from http://www.archive.org/stream/karankawaindian00olivgoog/karankawaindian00olivgoog_djvu.txt.

Gershenson, A. (2007). Las tortillas y el maíz. *La Jornada.* Retrieved from http://www.jornada.unam.mx/2007/01/21/index.php?section=politica&arti-cle=015a1pol.

de Gortari, E. (1961). Filosofía de la prehistoria de México.

Diánoia, 7(7), 53–78. Retrieved from http://dianoia.filosoficas.unam.mx/info/1961/DIA61_DeGortari.pdf.

Hall, G. D. (2006). "Hunter-Gatherer Life along the Frio River in the South Texas Brush Country." Retrieved from http://www.texasbeyondhistory.net/choke/index.html.

Jennings, F. (n.d.). Popular chili queens graced San Antonio Plazas. *Journal of the Life and Culture of San Antonio.* Retrieved from http://www.uiw.edu/sanantonio/jen-ningschiliqueens.html.

Keegan, M. (2010). *Southwest Indian Cookbook.* Santa Fe: Clear Light Publishing.

Kenmotsu, N., and Dial, S. (2009). "Native Peoples of the Coastal Prairies and Marshlands in Early Historic Times." Retrieved from http://www.texasbeyondhistory.net/coast/peoples/.

———. (2006). "Native Peoples of the South Texas Plains during Early Historic Times." Retrieved from http://www.texasbeyondhistory.net/st-plains/peoples/index.html.

Kidder, B. (2009). "Shellfish." Retrieved from http://www.texasbeyondhistory.net/coast/nature/images/shellfish.html.

Krieger, A. (2002). *We Came Naked and Barefoot: The Journey of Cabeza de Vaca across North America.* Austin: University of Texas Press.

Lang, A. S., and Long, C. (n.d.). "Land Grants," *Handbook of Texas Online.* Texas State Historical Association. Retrieved from http://www.tshaonline.org/handbook/online/articles/mpl01. Accessed December 29, 2012.

La Vere, D. (2004). *The Texas Indians.* College Station: Texas A & M University Press.

Lipscomb, C. A. Karankawa Indians, *Handbook of Texas Online.* Texas State Historical Association. Retrieved from http://www.tshaonline.org/handbook/online/articles/bmk05. Accessed November 1, 2012.

Lira Saade, C. (2005). "Numeros: las tortillas." Retrieved from http://www.jornada.unam.mx/2005/01/17/002n-

1sec.html.

McGraw, A. (2003). *Origins of the Camino Real in Texas*. Retrieved from http://www.texasalmanac.com/topics/history/origins-camino-real-texas.

McKeever Furst, J. L. (2003). Food for the Gods—Or, You Are Who You Eat in Ancient Mexico. *Expedition, 45*(2), 26–29. Retrieved from http://www.penn.museum/documents/publications/expedition/PDFs/45-2/Food for the Gods.pdf.

Meléndez Rentería, N. P., Rodríguez Herrera, R., Silva Vázquez, R., and Nevárez Moorillon, G. V. (2009). El orégano mexicano. *CienciaCierta, 5*(20). Retrieved from http://www.postgradoeinvestigacion.uadec.mx/CienciaCierta/CC20/CC20oregano.html.

Montaño, M. (1992). "The History of Mexican Folk Foodways of South Texas: Street Vendors, Offal Foods, and Barbacoa de Cabeza." Ph.D. diss., University of Pennsylvania.

———. (2013). Interview by A. M. Medrano. Colorado Springs, CO, February 28.

Moore, J. H. (1994). Putting Anthropology Back Together Again: The Ethnogenetic Critique of Cladistic Theory. *American Anthropologist, 4*(94), 925–948.

Morell, S. F., and Enig, M. (2000). *Guts and Grease: The Diet of Native Americans*. Retrieved from http://www.westonaprice.org/traditional-diets/guts-and-grease.

Newcomb, W. W. (1961). *The Indians of Texas from Prehistoric to Modern Times*. Austin: University of Texas Press.

Paredes, R. (2012). "Teaching Chicano Literature: An Historical Approach." Retrieved from http://www9.georgetown.edu/faculty/bassr/tamlit/essays/chicano.html.

Pilcher, J. M. (2012). *Planet Taco: A Global History of Mexican Food*. New York: Oxford University Press.

Poder Edomex. (2012). "Representa planta 'Pericón' recurso terapéutico y alimentício." Universidad Autónoma del Estado de México. Retrieved from http://poderedomex.com/notas.asp?id=54196.

Potter, D. (n.d.). "The Bedrock Mortars of Enchanted Rock." Retrieved from http://www.texasbeyondhistory.net/plateaus/images/ap16.html.

Ribeiro, S. (2012). "El maíz transgénico en México: químicamente toxico." Retrieved from http://www.reygal.com.mx/wordpress/index.php/2012/02/el-maiz-transgenico-en-mexico-quimicamente-toxico/.

Sánchez, O., Medellín, R., and Aldama, A. (2007). *Método de Evaluación del Riesgo de Extinción de las Especies Silvestres en México*. México, D.F.: Instituto Nacional de Ecología. Retrieved from http://www.ine.gob.mx/publicaciones/download/534.pdf

Sánchez-Colín, S., Mijares-Oviedo, P., López-López, L., and Barrientos-Priego, A. (2001). Historia del aguacate en México. *Cictamex 1998–2001*. Retrieved from http://avocadosource.com/journals/cictamex/cictamex_1998–2001/cictamex_1998–2001_pg_171–187.pdf.

Santibañez, R. (2007). *Rosa's New Mexican Table*. New York: Artisan.

Silva, N., and Nelson, D. (2004). The chili queens of San Antonio (radio series episode). In *Hidden Kitchens*. Washington, D.C.: National Public Radio. Retrieved from http://www.npr.org/templates/story/story.php?storyId=4107830.

Solis, F., and Gallegos, A. (2000). El mercado de Tlatelolco. *Pasajes de la Historia No. 1: El reino de Moctezuma*. Retrieved from http://www.mexicodesconocido.com.mx/el-mercado-de-tlatelolco.html.

Speller, C. F., Kemp, B. M., Lipe, W. D., and Yang, D. Y. (2010). "Ancient Mitochondrial DNA Analysis Reveals Complexity of Indigenous North American Turkey Domestication." Retrieved from http://www.pnas.org/content/early/2010/01/21/0909724107.full.pdf html?with-ds=yes.

Sperry, J. E. (2007). "Ethnogenesis of the Metis, Cree and Chippewa in Twentieth-Century Montana." Master's thesis, University of Montana.

Starchannel Communications. (n.d.). "Hispanic Demographics Overview." Retrieved from http://www.starchannel.

com/hispanic_demographics.html.

Straus, R. R. (2012). "Starbucks Bows to Vegan Pressure and Stops Using Crushed Insects for Dye in Drinks." Retrieved from http://www.dailymail.co.uk/news/article-2132645/Starbucks-bows-vegan-pressure-stops-using-crushed-insects-dye-drinks.html.

Texas State Historical Association. (1988). *The Texas Almanac: Religion in Early Texas*. Retrieved from http://www.texasalmanac.com/topics/history/religion-early-texas.

Thoms, A. (2012). *Learning from Cabeza de Vaca*. Retrieved from http://www.texasbeyondhistory.net/cabeza-cooking/index.html.

The Tonkawa Tribe of Oklahoma. (2012). *Tonkawa Tribal History*. Retrieved from http://www.tonkawatribe.com/history.htm.

Ustunol, Z. (2009). "Processed Cheese: What Is That Stuff Anyway?" Retrieved from https://www.msu.edu/user/mdr/vol14no2/ustunol.html.

Wilson, D. (2012). "Bioarchaeological Evidence of Subsistence Strategies among the East Texas Caddo." In *The Archaeology of the Caddo*, edited by T. K. Perttula and C. P. Walker, 86–116. Lincoln: University of Nebraska Press.

LIST OF RECIPES

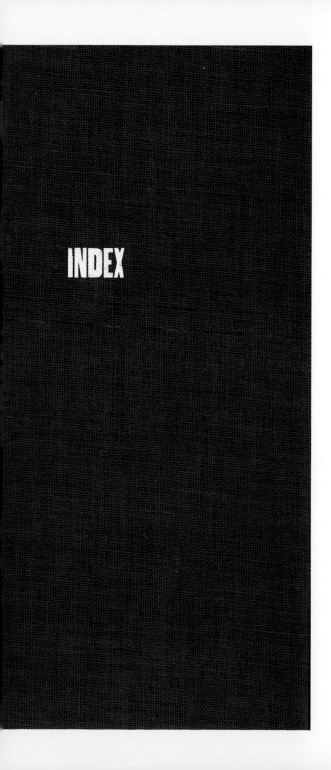

INDEX

Page numbers in italic refer to illustrations.

183

Index

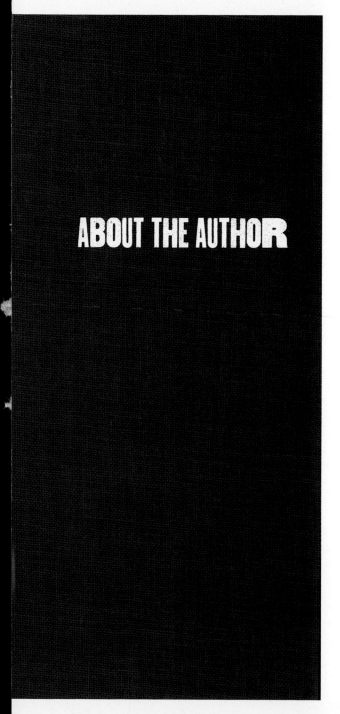

ABOUT THE AUTHOR

Chef and food writer Adán Medrano holds a Certificate in Culinary Arts from the Culinary Institute of America. He grew up in San Antonio, Texas, and in northern Mexico, where he developed his expertise in the flavor profile and techniques of indigenous Texas Mexican food.